The Adult Side
of Dyslexia

By the same author

Dyslexia and Spelling
Making Sense of It All
Kelli Sandman-Hurley
ISBN 978 1 98592 791 1
eISBN 978 1 78450 760 2

Dyslexia Advocate!
How to Advocate for a Child with Dyslexia
within the Public Education System
Kelli Sandman-Hurley
ISBN 978 1 84905 737 0
eISBN 978 1 78450 274 4

of related interest

Self-Fulfilment with Dyslexia
A Blueprint for Success
Margaret D. Malpas MBE
ISBN 978 1 78592 198 8
eISBN 978 1 78450 472 4

The Bigger Picture Book of Amazing
Dyslexics and the Jobs They Do
Kate Power and Kathy Iwanczak Forsyth
Foreword by Paul Smith
ISBN 978 1 78592 584 9
eISBN 978 1 78592 585 6

The Adult Side of Dyslexia

Kelli Sandman-Hurley

Jessica Kingsley Publishers
London and Philadelphia

First published in Great Britain in 2022 by Jessica Kingsley Publishers
An Hachette Company

1

The fonts, layout and overall design of this book have been prepared
according to dyslexia friendly principles. At JKP we aim to make
our books' content accessible to as many readers as possible.

A CIP catalogue record for this title is available from
the British Library and the Library of Congress

ISBN 978 1 78775 475 1
eISBN 978 1 78775 476 8

Printed and bound in the United States by West Publishing Corp

Trigger Warning: This book mentions suicide

Jessica Kingsley Publishers' policy is to use papers that are natural,
renewable and recyclable products and made from wood grown in
sustainable forests. The logging and manufacturing processes are expected
to conform to the environmental regulations of the country of origin.

Jessica Kingsley Publishers
Carmelite House
50 Victoria Embankment
London EC4Y 0DZ

www.jkp.com

This is dedicated to every single person who has ever struggled in school. To everyone who hid under a desk to avoid reading. To everyone who ran out of the classroom to avoid reading out loud. To everyone who still hopes no one will find out about their dyslexia. To all the adults who trusted me to do the right thing with their stories. I know it was hard and sometimes painful. Your tears and trembling voices did not go unnoticed—I hope I took good care of them.

Acknowledgements

A special thank you to my dad for reading everything I write and being critical, in a good way. To my mom for being supportive and always proud of me. To Talia and Olivia for doing the tedious work for me. To Stephen and Stacey for being my sounding boards.

To Rick and Casey for absolutely everything.

Contents

Preface

> Plain and simple, dyslexia is a major pain in the butt. I don't know how else to describe it. **Natalee**

To advocate means to add your voice. That is what the adults with dyslexia did when they sat down to be interviewed for this book. They added their voice to the discussion about dyslexia. They filled a void in the dyslexia discussion. They did so to try to make the dyslexic experience better for someone else.

For me, this book was a passion project. It was written in response to my experience as an adult literacy professional and all of the adults I met during that journey. As I left the adult literacy world and ventured into the world of children with dyslexia, and their families, the adults I met continued to be the driving force that kept me going and a constant reminder that children with dyslexia become adults with dyslexia. I often notice that those with dyslexia are not sought out for their opinions on topics like reading, writing, spelling instruction, and teaching practices. I also noticed that the social/emotional health of students struggling with reading and spelling is absent from instructional approaches. Their voices may not be muted, but they are definitely muffled.

This book was written for anyone with dyslexia who wants/ needs to know that they are not alone and that there are many, many adults who shared their story. It was written for parents who are trying to understand how their children are feeling. And it was written for educators, policy makers, advocates, school administrators, corporate trainers, bosses, judges, justice system employees, and anyone else who needs to understand how to accommodate for, and empathize with, the adults with dyslexia in their lives.

These stories remind us all that the words we use matter, the programs we use matter, the decisions we make about instruction matters, and yes, spelling matters. More often than not, we are making decisions about people with dyslexia without asking for their input. We don't ask for their guidance. We forget that they may have experienced school-induced trauma, and we have to understand how that has affected them in adulthood.

The chapters

How Would You Describe Your Dyslexia? In this chapter, the adults share how they talk about their dyslexia, revealing that they describe it as an experience, not a clinical diagnosis. Their descriptions are compared with how the education system defines dyslexia, and points are made about the discrepancy between the two descriptions and the advantages of creating a definition that encompasses both the clinical definition and the experience.

Dyslexia Hurts Dyslexia affects so much more than reading and spelling. In fact, struggles with reading and spelling affect behavior and that behavior often masks the pain the student is trying to hide. This chapter shares how dyslexia manifests in physical and behavioral symptoms and how those symptoms are often misunderstood.

Dyslexia-Induced Distrust Many adults with dyslexia have children themselves and when they notice reading and spelling difficulties in their own children, they often have anxiety and fear about having to return to a school to help their children get the services they need. They also have distrust of any education system that prevents them pursuing education and job advancement as adults. This chapter highlights how that distrust from childhood has prevented so many adults from attaining their goals.

Traumatic Teaching Practices Some everyday teaching practices may seem harmless but to the student with dyslexia, they can be traumatizing. In this chapter the adults describe the long-lasting effects of having to read out loud in front of their peers, which is often described as traumatic.

Is Spelling Important to You? Just about every adult with dyslexia will report that they still struggle with spelling, yet often they are not taught spelling because it is deemed unimportant or an issue that can be remedied by technology. This chapter provides evidence that spelling does matter, and the adults share stories about how poor spelling has affected them.

Do You Think Dyslexia is a Gift? This chapter examines the popular narrative that dyslexia is a gift and that people with dyslexia have inherent talents that will lead them to success. The adults share their opinions about that narrative, based on their own experiences.

Has Dyslexia Affected Your Ability to Succeed? In an effort to shine a more positive light on the experience of those with dyslexia, the dyslexia community shares a lot of positive stories about adults who have been very successful. In this chapter, the adults share how dyslexia has either prevented them from achieving success or has, indeed, helped them become successful. However, they attribute their success to hard work, advocacy, and determination, describing their success as being despite dyslexia, not because of it.

Acknowledge, Advocate, and Accommodate In the previous chapters, adults shared their experiences, their stories, and their opinions about their school and work experiences. In this chapter, practical strategies for adults with dyslexia, parents, teachers, and researchers are suggested that are based on the stories and opinions of the adults with dyslexia.

Education terminology

This book uses US terminology for school classes (kindergarten is equivalent to ages 5–6, first grade to ages 6–7, and so on, through to twelfth grade, which is equivalent to ages 17–18).

Introduction

Around third grade I had teachers put me in corners with a dunce cap on my head, send me to the office and so forth. Other teachers said I couldn't do that [referring to a goal he had] because I would have to learn to read first to do anything in my life. **Eddie**

I met Leonard in 1998. Leonard greeted me with a beaming smile and a hearty handshake. He was a tall, slender Jamaican man who had found his way to the adult literacy program of the San Diego Public Library where I was working. As we got acquainted, we chatted about his day and the weather as we walked back to the small office that we used to assess incoming students. When we sat down and I started organizing my papers, I noticed Leonard was sitting across the table from me and hanging his head while waiting for me to give him directions. I proceeded to ask him questions about his background and literacy issues. After about three or four questions, Leonard began to sob, really sob. He shared how his life had been so negatively impacted by his literacy struggles and that he was currently struggling to survive. He shared that he had been ostracized from his family in

Jamaica because he could not read or spell, and his siblings were academically successful—so he was expendable. He found his way to the adult literacy program when he had not been able to pass a test at work in order to get a raise. He was terrified and terribly embarrassed that he might not be able to support his own family. He told me all of this through tears and an incredible amount of shame. I was the first person he had ever told, and with that information, I knew I had just been given the responsibility to make sure his revelation was acknowledged and rewarded.

> **After about three or four questions, Leonard began to sob, really sob. He shared how his life had been so negatively impacted by his literacy struggles and that he was currently struggling to survive.**

The most important thing Leonard taught me that day, as have all the adults with dyslexia I have met since, was that what he needed before I did any assessing or teaching was acknowledgement and understanding. He needed to tell his story. He needed to tell it to someone who understood. He needed me to acknowledge his pain and his experience. He needed to understand why he struggled and be assured that it was not his fault, because no amount of effort or motivation can overcome the academic symptoms of dyslexia in the absence of appropriate teaching and accommodations.

Leonard had internalized the messages that he needed to try harder, that he wasn't motivated enough, and that he was not smart. While those things may not have been said to him in so many words, they were communicated in thinly veiled comments by educators and family members, body language, facial expressions, and failed attempts at various reading programs.

Leonard ended up working one-on-one with his volunteer tutor at the adult literacy program for many years, and he accomplished many of his goals. The longer he stayed, the bigger his smile was and the higher he held his head. He was no longer ashamed, and he truly believed he was capable of learning. His perseverance and his motivation speak volumes about his intelligence. He eventually did get a promotion and was much more confident in helping his children with schoolwork.

> **Leonard ended up working one-on-one with his volunteer tutor at the adult literacy program for many years, and he accomplished many of his goals. The longer he stayed, the bigger his smile was and the higher he held his head. He was no longer ashamed, and he truly believed he was capable of learning.**

Leonard was a man who had undiagnosed dyslexia. He never had an intervention. He never had access to accommodations. He believed it was his fault and he believed he needed to try harder. He did not have home support. He did not have school support. Dyslexia occurs on a severity continuum from mild, to moderate, to severe, to profound, and Leonard was on the severe side of the dyslexia continuum. He did not have an advocate. He, like so many of the adults in this book, was a victim of his education. But he is also a success story because despite the internalization of those negative messages that he was not smart, he simultaneously knew that he could succeed.

Leo eventually worked his way out of his own shame, but it shouldn't have happened the way it did. It was not his fault. However, like the adults in this book, his life path was changed by his school experience. The school experience may have altered his life path, it may have altered his self-esteem, it may have altered his confidence, but the experience did not prevent him from trying to better his life, and he continued to work for what he knew he was capable of achieving. Leonard was a casualty of a school system that, to this day, generally does not take dyslexia seriously enough to prevent more stories like his.

> **His story mattered to the state senators more than facts and figures and magnified the need for people with dyslexia to be at every meeting, every table, and every conversation about dyslexia.**

Then there was Max. In 2015, I was one of the expert witnesses for the California Assembly Bill 1369 which helped schools identify dyslexia. After I gave my testimony, which included facts and figures about dyslexia and my opinion, based on those facts and figures, about how we can help dyslexic students, a brave young man named Max began his testimony about the experience of being dyslexic in the school system. As he spoke, I watched how the state senators listened to his story in a way they had not listened to my testimony. I watched as they subtly wiped tears from their faces, as did I, as Max spoke. Max stole the show because what he had to say was far more important than what I had to say. He stood up not just for himself, but also for so many kids who could not advocate for themselves. His story mattered to the state senators more than facts and figures and magnified the need for people with dyslexia to be at every meeting, every table, and every conversation about dyslexia.

> **Max stole the show because what he had to say was far more important than what I had to say. He stood up not just for himself, but also for so many kids who could not advocate for themselves.**

Any parent or advocate of a dyslexic child will tell you that the experience of struggling readers and spellers, dyslexics, is not taken seriously enough. The education system doesn't act fast enough. It waits for the student to fail for several years before it deems the situation "severe enough" to provide special education services. It waits for the student to "catch up" or "grow out of it." It even waits for the student to just find a book they like. The long-term impact of waiting for the student to change isn't understood, nor how delayed identification and intervention affects a person—for the rest of their life.

People in the education system might think they understand, and they may be doing the best they can, but the current system is accountable for the lifelong consequences of their actions and their inactions. In fact, every time there is a delay, a denial, a lack of awareness, and/or a lack of services, a piece of that student's self-esteem and potential falls away. Every year that passes is more time to internalize school failures and self-blame, and the shame grows. Their anxiety increases.

> **Every time there is a delay, a denial, a lack of awareness, and/or a lack of services, a piece of that student's self-esteem and potential falls away.**

That is what this book is about: listening to the stories and learning from them. During my work with adults who struggle with their reading and spelling, I have heard some pretty horrifying and heartbreaking stories. I have sat with numerous adults who have cried while recounting memories of the daily school struggle. Some of them are tormented because they can't understand why they did not succeed in school and how and why they became a casualty of the educational system. They want to know why they were left to their own devices, forced to wait for help, and passed along from grade to grade with no real help of any kind—they feel educationally expendable, which means that it seems to be acceptable to have a certain percentage of students who will not succeed academically and it's acceptable to deny them the specific help dyslexia requires. There isn't enough time and resources for those who do not perform like the non-dyslexic students.

We put so much trust in strangers every day. We trust those who prepare our food to take precautions while cooking and handling it. We trust airline pilots to get us to our destinations safely. We trust doctors to cure our illnesses. We trust educators to teach all of our children. We assume all of these people are sufficiently trained. The difference is that if a driver or pilot is careless, their own lives are also at stake and the end result is a sensational and newsworthy catastrophe; in the end, there is always someone to blame. But the education community has become careless with our struggling students and the casualties (dyslexic students) leave the system quietly—no news story to tell their harrowing stories.

After I listened to the adults' stories and subsequently read the transcripts, I became acutely aware of how isolating the dyslexic experience can be and how what happens to some kids, without much more than an uncomfortable Individualized Education Program (IEP) meeting every once in a while, is almost criminal. Lawsuits come and go, and many parents who are altruistic think their lawsuit will help more children than just their own, but that is usually not the case. The squeaky wheel usually only helps one child. We put our trust in a system that allows our children to twist in the wind, forgetting or ignoring the long-term effects of unidentified dyslexia, late identification of dyslexia, and/or inappropriate intervention, without ever being held accountable in any meaningful way. If a plane crashes, the airline is held accountable. If lettuce is contaminated and people get sick, the catering company is held accountable. If a child fails to learn to read or spell, the school system blames the child or the parent—that is the purest form of injustice.

> **Parents can be steamrolled in these meetings and even though they know their children better than anyone, they still feel powerless and lost in the power structure of the education system.**

As a dyslexia advocate, I have witnessed everything first-hand in dozens of IEP meetings. I have witnessed teachers telling parents to read more to their children. I have heard children being labeled with a lack of motivation to learn to read. I have seen children of color being labeled with behavior issues instead of digging deeper into the reason for the behavior. Parents can be steamrolled in these meetings, and even though they know their children better than anyone, they still feel powerless and lost in the power structure of the education system. Even worse are the parents who are left to advocate on their own for a plethora of valid reasons. For those parents, I wrote the book *Dyslexia Advocate!* (2016) so that they could attend school meetings with enough information, and confidence, to defeat the myths and have a complete understanding of their rights. What I have learned in these meetings, and from listening to the stories of adults, is that the problem lies in a lack of empathy, a lack of sympathy, a lack of awareness about what dyslexia is and is not, and a lack of understanding of the very real emotional and practical consequences (work and school opportunities become limited) of dyslexia. Those families with resources and support fare far better than those without, and that's when it gets criminal. I've heard all the rhetoric in the dyslexia community about the positive aspect of dyslexia but my experience in adult literacy told me differently. This philosophy is really only applicable to the more fortunate among us, and as my interviews progressed, that idea was confirmed, in spades—it is not perceived as a "gift" by the majority of those who have it.

> They pushed me to the side. They said I'd get to you later or whatnot. Then when the time come [sic] and I ask for help again you go and make me sit down. I feel like you pushed me to the side. **Charles**

> **What I have learned in these meetings, and from listening to the stories of adults, is that the problem lies in a lack of empathy, a lack of sympathy, a lack of awareness about what dyslexia is and is not, and a lack of understanding of the very real emotional and practical consequences of dyslexia.**

Some of what I write about will seem obvious, but when you stop and think that these stories are still told today by kids in school, it seems that the obviousness isn't changing how we do things. Schools are still waiting too long to identify, to provide appropriate services, to provide accommodations, and they are still trying a little of this and a little of that type of instruction to see what will stick. In fact, a few of the adults mentioned that they were mortified to be not only the kid with dyslexia, but also the kid wearing colored lenses and maybe even having to go to questionable therapy where they crawled on the floor. The educational system is still waiting for the student to fit the instruction, instead of fitting the instruction to the student.

Meet the adults

I met the majority of the adults on Zoom for about an hour. In some cases, I followed up with their parents via email. I also met with others in person at a coffee shop. I met the inmates at a California state prison. I recorded each session and asked each adult the same questions, which I then transcribed. Once all of the interviews were complete, I read through the transcripts to identify common themes, which I am reporting in this book.

Every interview was emotional. Some adults were nervous, some were angry. Some weren't sure if they could trust me and some really needed to tell their story. For many adults, the interview was cathartic, and many said at the end of our interview that, "It was really good to talk about this."

The adults in this book could be described the following way: a teacher/s, a philosopher, an opera singer, a prison inmate, an Academy Award winner, an accomplished artist, a mom, a college student, a nurse, an athlete, an office worker, a supervisor, a mathematician, a personal trainer, a dad, a park ranger, an engineer, a chef, a project manager, a bus driver, a home healthcare worker, an insurance agent, a software engineer. To name just a few. They were Caucasian, black, and Latino. They were younger, older. Some were employed, some were unemployed, and several were underemployed. They were American, Canadian, British, Australian, and Irish. They came from all walks of life, representing the wealthy, destitute, and middle class. What they all have in common is dyslexia; what they don't have in common is how the external forces in their lives have shaped their dyslexic experiences and their perspectives.

Although I am not able to share all of their stories individually in this book, each of their stories plays a significant role in the book, and I would like to thank each one of them here. So, thank you for your patience with my questions, patience with my internet connection, and mostly, thank you for your trust in me. Thank you to: Adam, Amy T., Amy W., Angela, Anthony, Arte, Ashley, Beth, Beth, Bob, Cary, Charles, Christa, Claudia, Chuck, Denisha, Earl, Eddie, Edward, Erin, Faith, Gwen, Hannah, James, Jamie, Jean, Josh, Kate, Katie, Kendall, Lois, Margaret, Maryann, Martin, Melissa, Missy, Natalee, Neice, Nick, Nicole, Peggy, Philomena, Riley, Russell, Sean, Stacey, Stephen, Stephanie, Suz, Tannis, Tim, Tom, and Will.

> **What the adults in this book all have in common is dyslexia; what they don't have in common is how the external forces in their lives have shaped their dyslexic experiences and their perspectives.**

A pandemic happened

When I started the interviews for this book, the world was humming along like normal. Kids were in school, and people were travelling, attending concerts, weddings, and working as usual. I was very intent on making sure that voices from all walks of life were included in this book, and I was excited that I had been granted access to a few California prisons to interview inmates, get tours of their education facilities, even talk with some of their teachers. The first visit was so impactful on me that I was very much looking forward to the next two visits, but Covid-19 hit and the prison visits were cancelled indefinitely. As I finish this book, the pandemic continues to prevent me from including more of those voices, but I have been able to draw from experience with adults at the adult literacy program who had previously been incarcerated and the interviews I was able to complete before the pandemic. I think it is important to point this out, because their dyslexic experiences tend to be much different than the experiences of those who were able to successfully navigate adulthood and dyslexia. As soon as it is permissible, I will visit those prisons so that their voices can be included in my future work in some way.

Terminology in this book

A word can be so much more than a word—it can divide, and it can unite. A word that is perceived as being misused can stop someone from listening to anything after the word was uttered. The word dyslexia is so misused in popular culture and education programs that the mere utterance of the word can be as divisive as a political conversation. Sometimes, just saying the word dyslexia can bring a school meeting to a screeching halt. I have heard a parent suggest that their child has dyslexia during a school meeting and then heard the entire team make false statements , such as, "Dyslexia isn't real, we don't work with dyslexia," and suggest that the student is just a reluctant reader. They replaced the word dyslexia with reluctant.

As a presenter, one thing that always seems to be on the minds of workshop participants is the language that I use. Some people want me to use the "person-first" terminology and some want me to use the term dyslexic. In order to find out what is actually the most appropriate, I asked adults. I asked them how they would like to be described. I wanted to know whether they preferred Joe with dyslexia or Joe the dyslexic. The overwhelming majority responded that they didn't care what they were called as long as the word "dyslexia" was used in some way, shape, or form. This gave me the permission to vacillate between dyslexic and person with dyslexia throughout this book.

> Some people want me to use the "person-first" terminology and some want me to use the term dyslexic. I asked adults how they would like to be described. I wanted to know whether they preferred Joe with dyslexia or Joe the dyslexic. The overwhelming majority responded that they didn't care what they were called as long as the word "dyslexia" was used in some way, shape, or form. This gave me the permission to vacillate between dyslexic and person with dyslexia throughout this book.

In this book, I have been very careful with my word choices. I use the words many (many of the adults...), most (most of the adults...), some (some of the adults...), and all (all of the adults) very deliberately. The journeys of students with dyslexia are complex and are shaped by so many variables that it is important to clarify when a theme I think I uncovered during the interviews is ubiquitous or perhaps, for example, true for those with resources only.

The premise of this book is simple. It's about listening. Listening to the collective stories of a group of people who have a shared experience. It is about listening without judgment. It is about hearing the collective feelings of shame. It is about uncovering the implicit bias of the education system against these misunderstood students. It is about how that bias affected their daily lives. It is about understanding that the collective experience of these students is a far better indicator of what helps and what doesn't help than relying on individual stories. I went into this project expecting to hear some of the things I heard, but when I was finished, I was a different person because what they shared was often simultaneously heartbreaking and heart-warming. Their stories should give us all pause and help us rethink what we do for and what we say about dyslexics.

> I went into this project expecting to hear some of the things I heard, but when I was finished, I was a different person because what these dyslexic adults shared was often simultaneously heartbreaking and heart-warming.

Chapter 1

How Would You Describe Your Dyslexia?

> When you can't help but take your time, you have time to notice a lot. There is room for those most elementary and forceful words to linger, for connections across text to fall in place, and for pertinent questions to emerge and demand attention. When you have to labor to string the words in the right order, you cannot help but dwell upon and participate in the author's own sentence construction. You get to try out, and learn from, her approach to composition and expression. **Chuck**

I'm tall. I have always been tall. When I was in elementary school and middle school (age 5–14), I was always the tallest girl in the class. I was in the back of every group picture or on the top level of the riser. I didn't like being the tall girl. I heard all the jokes tall girls hear when they are young. I was very self-conscious about it. My parents were not particularly tall, and neither was my sister—so I didn't have anyone to commiserate with. My best friend at around 12 years old was taller than me—did we choose each other because we could relate to each other? It's entirely possible. I didn't appreciate my height until I started playing sports and was able to embrace my height and create something positive with it— although I would not consider it a gift, I do consider it an advantage. To this day, I enjoy being asked to get something off of a top shelf at a grocery store (which happens more than you might think).

If you look up the word tall in the dictionary you might get a definition like this: *of great or more than average height.* But my tallness was so much more than that. It was how others defined me for most of my childhood; it made me self-conscious; it created a need in me to sit in the back row, which I still do, to try not to stand out in a crowd; I even went so far as to hunch over so I wouldn't appear so tall. My tallness was an experience. No one ever asked me: what is it like to be tall, or how are you feeling about being tall? My tall experience was not the same as a tall experience for a boy.

Obviously, the consequences of being taller than everyone else cannot be equated to the experience of struggling at school on a day-to-day basis. So, what does being tall have to do with being a dyslexic adult? Well, dyslexia is an experience, and it's often whittled down to a clinical definition. While a definition is necessary, the dyslexic experience will be different for a female with dyslexia, a person of color with dyslexia, a poor child with dyslexia, a male with dyslexia, a rich person with dyslexia, and on and on. We have to take the time to stop and ask the child, the tween, the teenager, and the adult to describe their dyslexia. And when we ask that question, we have to listen, really listen, without trying to make their description fit the definition. We need to make the definition fit the description.

> **The dyslexic experience will be different for a female with dyslexia, a person of color with dyslexia, a poor child with dyslexia, a male with dyslexia, a rich person with dyslexia, and on and on.**

> You work incredibly hard for average results.   **Lois**

"How would you describe your dyslexia?" was the first question I asked all 50+ of the adults I spoke to and I received 50+ different responses. However, what each of those responses had in common was that they described an experience, not a list of symptoms. The way Chuck, a soft-spoken man who was also a doctoral student in philosophy, describes his dyslexia is so interesting because he attributes his ability to read the text more closely to his dyslexia. He believes his slow, laborious reading and rereading helps him to comprehend deeply what he reads. That would be important for an educator working with Chuck to know. Neice, a recent high-school graduate who was just starting college, describes it as a block that she hasn't been able to overcome. How do we help Neice if we don't know how she views her dyslexia? We have to talk with her about her block before we start teaching. But we have to ask her to find out.

> **The way Chuck, a soft-spoken man who was also a doctoral student in philosophy, describes his dyslexia is so interesting because he attributes his ability to read the text more closely to his dyslexia. He believes his slow, laborious reading and rereading helps him to comprehend deeply what he reads.**

The adults in this book, without fail, described dyslexia as an experience, an emotion, a feeling, and/or a traumatic event that occurred every day they had to go to school. On the following two pages, you will see a sample of how they described their dyslexia:

When I was younger, I didn't know I had dyslexia, so I used to go under the desk and cry for my mama around certain subjects. So about third grade, I realized, I had—well, they told me I had dyslexia. **Denisha**

It's a lot of concentration. **Katie**

I always viewed myself as the stupid slow kid who just couldn't read or spell. I had minimal self-worth from an academic perspective, which quickly spilled over into the personal areas of my life, which in turn affected many of the choices I made, many resulting in negative behaviors—Stacey

Trying to sound out words was such a nightmare. **Hannah**

It's a block and I will get over it by next year or something like that by practicing on it. **Neice**

Well, it's been really hard. I was in special education all of my school years. Got all the way to the eleventh grade. Dropped out because I couldn't pass none of the tests that they were giving out. I just felt like I couldn't do it of my reading. Dropped out of school. Tried to go back several times and it's just not working for me. I would get so far on the reading and everything and then I would just quit. I would just give up. **Gwen**

It was very difficult for me in school with teachers and administrators and early I think I was labeled a behavior problem. I know that is a very common thing. **Earl**

I have to reread a lot. I'll be reading and then I wouldn't even know what I was reading. **Beth**

I would describe it—I would say, my biggest problem is I can read, but I won't know what I'm reading. **Tannis**

I thought I was retarded. **Melissa**

I remember looking at the words on the page and wished I could read and understand them. I would have to read a page over ten times before I could piece together the meaning of the words so I could understand what I was reading. I would struggle to spell basic words. Reading was slow and painful. I remember pretending to read books, just so I could look like I could read. **Amy T.**

You struggle every day. **Tom**

My earliest memory of school struggles would be in first grade. Kindergarten was a play time and I enjoyed the social activities and arts and crafts. In first grade we started to write and read. My friends were smart and catching on to what the teacher was asking us to do, but the instructions didn't make sense to me. I was shy and quiet and didn't want to be called on. As I moved on through the grades, I don't remember much because I blocked most of the memories that were painful. I was called stupid by teachers and peers. My nickname became "Amy Lame," my middle name was Lane. I remember being told to do various activities by teachers and thinking, "I know I am not stupid, but I can't do what they are asking." I was put on the non-college track very early on and told I wouldn't amount to much. I was an easy crier and felt very frustrated and confused and didn't like school.   **Amy T.**

The language used by the adults to describe dyslexia often included nuances of feeling inadequate in the classroom and feeling like no one understood them as young students. They used language that reflected the everyday, exhausting struggle they faced in school. For the most part, they expressed that no one had ever really asked them to describe it and very rarely did anyone talk with them about it as children.

Their feelings of being misunderstood are validated by the language education professionals use when they describe dyslexia—which is clinical and diagnostic, and is whittled down to a list of symptoms. The problem with this is that it ends up being too clinical to use in the classroom. The student becomes a list of symptoms and we are not treating, or acknowledging, the experience. This disconnect may be a major contributor to the isolation and frustration a student with dyslexia can experience—they are misunderstood. We have to treat the emotion alongside the reading and spelling.

We rely so heavily on numbers. We look to standardized testing to help us understand the strengths and weaknesses of struggling students, and that information can be helpful, mostly to identify dyslexia and determine where to begin, as well as to measure progress. To date, that quantitative data seems to be the main force behind the definitions that are used. But there is a significant lack, or oversight, of qualitative research, like the research in this book, to support and humanize the quantitative results in reading science.

But we rarely ask people with dyslexia, even as very young children, to describe for us what works and what doesn't work. Young children know they are struggling; if they cannot describe it, we can get creative with helping them communicate their experience to us. We can describe dyslexia and ask if that is what they are experiencing. But we can't ignore it. We don't treat them as a partner in the teaching process. We rarely take the time to sit and talk with them about literacy struggles and what they mean to them. Most of the adults shared that it would have been immensely helpful if someone had had an honest conversation about what dyslexia is as soon as it was identified. Those who did not have it identified as children would have loved to have someone at least acknowledge their effort and their intellect.

Most of the adults shared that it would have been immensely helpful if someone had had an honest conversation about what dyslexia is as soon as it was identified. Those who did not have it identified as children would have loved to have someone at least acknowledge their effort and their intellect

Dyslexia symptoms

- Difficulty decoding words in isolation.

- Difficulty spelling (orthography).

- Difficulty with phonemic awareness: Phonemic awareness is the ability of the student to verbally manipulate language before graphemes are presented. ("A grapheme is a letter, or a group of letters, that represent a phoneme. In the word *chip* there are four letters: c, h, i, p and three graphemes: ch - i - p. In the word *chips*, there are five letters: c, h, i, p, s and four graphemes: ch - i - p - s and two morphemes: chip + s" (Sandman-Hurley, 2019).)

- Difficulty with phonological awareness: Phonological awareness is the ability to analyze speech or spoken language, from identifying individual words, to word parts or syllables, and then into the smallest parts called phonemes or speech sounds (IDA, 2020).

- Slow, laborious reading: Children with dyslexia might read a passage or sentences very slowly, trying to decode (sound out) each and every word. This difficulty is more pronounced when larger, polysyllabic words are included in the text.

36

- Difficulty with math word problems: A child with dyslexia who is struggling with reading will also struggle to read math problems.

- Reversing letters past the second grade (age seven/ eight): The reversal of b and d, as well as other letters, is normal through the first grade (age six/ seven); after that it becomes a red flag.

To determine whether teachers understood dyslexia in the same way as dyslexics, I also asked teachers to describe dyslexia in their own words. Their answers, while mostly correct, boiled down to clinical symptoms void of human emotion. This isn't an opportunity to insult teachers, rather it's an opportunity to reflect and improve. Below is a sample of how some of the educators described dyslexia.

Dyslexia is a neurobiological condition. Children with dyslexia have a difficult time mapping our oral language to written language. They may also have difficulty with basic and advanced phonological skills.—Reading specialist, K-5 (kindergarten to fifth grade)

The part of the brain that is supposed to understand and interpret language does not work the same in dyslexics as with other people. ... When reading their brain may see a team of letters and may not immediately recognize what sound it makes.   —Reading interventionist, K-5 (kindergarten to fifth grade)

Dyslexia is a processing issue. It's how the brain takes in information. There are many different types. It is often seen in kids' reading and writing.   —Third-grade teacher

In 2002, the International Dyslexia Association (IDA) published its definition of dyslexia, which is the probably the most commonly used definition. It was necessary to create a definition for legal cases and for a clinical diagnosis. However, there is room for improvement by humanizing the definition, using the information from adults with dyslexia. There are striking differences between the IDA official definition of dyslexia and the way adult dyslexics describe it—much like the difference between the way adults with dyslexia describe it and teachers describe it. There is not a common language, and this could be alienating to adults and families who are describing the experience and pain, while the professionals are reducing it to clinical symptoms.

International Dyslexia Association (IDA) definition

Dyslexia is a specific learning disability that is neurobiological in origin. It is characterized by difficulties with accurate and/or fluent word recognition and by poor spelling and decoding abilities. These difficulties typically result from a deficit in the phonological component of language that is often unexpected in relation to other cognitive abilities and the provision of effective classroom instruction.

> Secondary consequences may include problems in reading comprehension and reduced reading experience that can impede growth of vocabulary and background knowledge. (IDA, 2021)

This discrepancy between how education professionals and dyslexics understand dyslexia amplifies for students, and their families, that their journeys, struggles, and experiences are inherently undervalued, misunderstood, or dysunderstood and that the need for dyslexia awareness remains high. Their life experiences and the amount of school trauma they have experienced matter when defining dyslexia, because those experiences will all impact which symptoms they exhibit and how they will respond to an intervention, which is why those experiences should be included in the definitions of dyslexia. For example, I had a student who was about 12 when we started to meet. He was bright, kind, and on the profound side of the dyslexia spectrum. At our second meeting, I noticed that he was not super engaged with me and was a little stand-offish. So, I pushed my materials to the side and just looked at him and said, "I know you think I am just another lady in a long line of ladies who think they can help you, is that right?" His face literally changed in that instant. He smirked and said, "Yes." We spent the next few sessions just talking about dyslexia, words, and language, and building rapport. Once he felt confident that I understood him, and that I might actually be able to help him, our sessions were productive. There was no way I was going to make progress if I didn't make the effort to address his previous experiences and his frustration.

> This discrepancy between how education professionals and dyslexics understand dyslexia amplifies for students, and their families, that their journeys, struggles, and experiences are inherently undervalued, misunderstood, or dysunderstood and that the need for dyslexia awareness remains high.

What did we learn?

- Adults with dyslexia do not view their dyslexia in the same way as educators and researchers.
- Any time there is a decision being made about how we describe those with dyslexia, there needs to be more adequate representation from the dyslexia community. That representation should include all walks of life, not just those who have succeeded on a grand scale.

Myth: Dyslexia isn't real.

Being a dyslexia denier isn't helpful to anyone. It's not helpful to the students, to the family, or to the school. In fact, identifying dyslexia and subsequently using the term, or the label, is liberating for both the dyslexic and the school because they have not only an explanation for their academic struggles, but also a much better idea of how to help. It's liberating because the student can stop blaming themselves or labeling themselves as stupid. Using other terms, like "reluctant reader," "poor responder," and "specific learning disabled," only allows for more inappropriate interventions to be used and delays to interventions and identification, which is what causes trauma. Remember, these kids become adults and what we do during school will stay with them forever. Dyslexia exists, no matter what you call it.

Chapter 2

Dyslexia Hurts

> It hurts. You get stomach aches and headaches. The back of my neck would start to burn when I had to read out loud. It hurts. **Josh**

When James came into the room, I was uncomfortable. I had never been to a prison before, and I wasn't sure which questions I would or should ask. I had decided to keep my questions to those about his school struggles. James was a young African American man. As I began asking James about his school experience and how his undiagnosed dyslexia had affected him, he told me a story about why he was in prison. He was arrested for stealing a car. He said he was unable to read what he was signing and thought he was signing an agreement for the car, which he wasn't. When I asked him if he thought he was in prison as a direct result of dyslexia, he emphatically said yes. As I pressed a bit more, he shared that he had several brothers and sisters, he had very little money, and his mom was not capable of helping him. His literacy struggles were never addressed by his family or his school. He shared his frustration with not being able to learn, not being able to get help, and basically not being given a chance to succeed. He had a young family of his own, and he was distraught about not being with them and worried about their literacy struggles. Being in prison is painful. Being away from family is painful. My heart breaks for James, and his journey should have been different. He should have been identified. He should have received help. He should be able to read well enough that he knows what he is signing. That should be his right.

Many adults, like James, remember school as being a daily struggle with embarrassment and failure. They feel isolated and rarely find someone at school who understands them or how to teach them. Some are lucky to have understanding parents or family members, but for many, that is not available. That frustration, anxiety, anger, and hopelessness can manifest in many ways. For some of the adults, they manifested as stomach aches, in others as anxiety, in others as what looks like indifference, and in still others as self-medicating. While dyslexia may not manifest as a behavioral problem or a physical disability that is visible, a person with dyslexia can experience pain. It's emotional pain, physical pain, and even social angst. They might avoid social situations where reading and/or spelling might happen publicly, such as church, neighborhood meetings, and recovery meetings.

> **Many adults, like James, remember school as being a daily struggle with embarrassment and failure. Some are lucky to have understanding parents or family members, but for many, that is not available. That frustration, anxiety, anger, and hopelessness can manifest in many ways. For some of the adults, they manifested as stomach aches, in others as anxiety, in others as what looks like indifference, and in still others as self-medicating.**

A majority of the adults who were interviewed shared feelings of believing they were "stupid" as children. While they no longer believe that, they still carry the shame from not measuring up to their potential.

A majority of the adults who were interviewed shared feelings of believing they were "stupid" as children. While they no longer believe that, they still carry the shame from not measuring up to their potential.

The constant message is that you are not good enough.   Lois

Peggy's story is almost the polar opposite to James's. Hers is an example of the difference that not only resources, but also understanding, from at least one adult, can have on the trajectory of a dyslexic student. Before I met Peggy, I was nervous. I knew of her presence in the dyslexia community, and I knew she was passionate about helping other dyslexics. I knew that she was incredibly accomplished in her professional life, but I made an effort not to read too much about her before I met her, so I would not form any preconceived notions. During our conversation, she shared that she was identified very early in her academic career and that she was lucky that a family friend was well versed in an approach that is appropriate for dyslexic students and offered to help her. She had the resources to attend schools that were attentive to her individual needs. She had home support and resources to provide for her education. However, she was quick to point out that even though she was lucky and she had support, her struggle was, and is, still difficult and should not be discounted:

> It took a while to feel that my story had value because at first, I felt like, well, you were so lucky. You got help. You got to go to good schools. You came from a background where your parents could afford the help. You didn't have to work three jobs in order to go to college, which would have killed me because I had to spend so much extra time doing everything. I could not have actually physically done that. Right? I couldn't have gotten the work done because all the work took me three times longer. So I felt like, well, what is the point of telling my story because I'm the 1 percent. But then I realized, no, the point is with all the help that I got look at how hard it still was and is and all the baggage I still had.   **Peggy**

She still doubts herself, and she still works extra hard to do what comes easily to so many others, even with the extraordinary help she had. While James went to prison, Peggy eventually went on to earn the highest honor in her professional field, an Academy Award. There are two stories in the dyslexic world: one is the story that happens when a student is unidentified, unsupported, and unaccommodated, and the other happens when a student is identified, supported, and accommodated.

The day-to-day of attending school was described as traumatic by nearly all of the adults interviewed. I asked them to describe what school was like when they were young. Some of the answers below do describe how frustration, embarrassment, fatigue, and anger manifest themselves in the classroom:

> I'd cry getting on the school bus. I didn't want to go. Then when I'd get to school, I would fake being sick and they'd come pick me up. **Tom**

> I was in third grade and I would get stomach aches before English. **Melissa**

> I had this drowning feeling. Like I couldn't keep my head above water. **Ashley**

> I remember going home almost every day just feeling sick because I was always being put down. **Suz**

> It was very torturous when I was younger. I mean because you're just in fear the whole time of them calling on you to read. Or I was just—when they said, "All right we're going to read," I would start sweating, I would start getting nauseous like I said, and it's even if I'm sitting there and I'm counting, I'm sitting there scared to death when it comes to my turn to read. **Will**

Decades ago, Maslow (1943) created a hierarchy illustrating what most of us probably instinctually know about what students need before they can learn. The hierarchy included the lowest level of basic needs (like food and shelter), safety, love and belongingness, esteem, and finally self-actualization. So many of the adults felt emotionally unsafe at school, which limited their ability to move beyond that tier. Most of the adults reported feeling different, isolated, and stupid, and that they didn't belong. For the most part, the exceptions to this were the students who were successful athletes. Most of the students never felt they achieved mastery or the respect of their peers in school, which left them unable to attain the top tier, self-actualization, which is when a student has realized their potential.

> I used to go to the doctor's office a lot because my parents thought I had chest pains. I was stressed out.   **Tom**

> **So many of the adults felt emotionally unsafe at school. Most of the adults reported feeling different, isolated, and stupid, and that they didn't belong.**

John Hicks (2019) explained the impact of feeling unsafe in the most perfect way:

> If a dyslexic child doesn't feel safe within school and somehow is unable to get out of the vicious circle of struggling to keep up, showing behaviour to mask those challenges and teachers not having the insight to see beyond the behaviour and looking to nurture, our children will feel isolated from their peers and lose hope in their ability to attain (Esteem) and ultimately hinder the development of their own potential (self-actualisation).

This beautiful description underscores the need to address the feelings of failure, low self-esteem, and frustration before, and during, any intervention. The feelings could lead to behavioral issues, which could lead to misdiagnoses of attention issues. According to Maslow, it is difficult for a child, or anyone, to learn without positive esteem. So, when we take a child out of class and just start going down a checklist of skills to be taught, we have completely ignored the fact that they are not ready to absorb that information. Hicks (2019) goes on to describe the consequences of ignoring this stage of Maslow's hierarchy in the following way:

> Poor self-esteem is so often hidden but without intervention could lead to further problems with overwhelm, confidence, and anxiety which could ultimately lead to challenges with mental health as a child goes into adulthood and struggles to cope with the day to day challenges of life.

The quotes from adults with dyslexia on page 45 included all of those feelings and experiences—they needed an emotional intervention before a reading intervention could possibly be effective. That type of intervention will only happen when the education system has professionals who have developed knowledge about dyslexia and empathy for those with dyslexia. This means that they understand not only the clinical symptoms of dyslexia, but also the social/emotional impact.

Waiting for a child to outgrow their dyslexia, mature, or find a book they like are all forms of blaming the child. It is not the child who needs to change, it is the intervention.

We also need to take care to make sure that the programs and approaches we choose for dyslexic students are appropriate. This is paramount because every time they "fail to respond" to intervention, they internalize it as their personal failure—that's painful. This "failure to respond" also creates shame. Shame was another word that surfaced many times during these interviews. Their shame was a result of not being able to perform academically like their peers.

I was like "You people have tried and tried to bring me up to an appropriate level on reading, writing and spelling and it's not going to happen." So, I've got to figuring out strategies to deal with that... My success story is that I told you guys to screw off, and I went and figured out things on my own. Cary

When I was little, I felt, because I didn't understand it, so I felt like I was weird and different. Tannis

Speaking of interventions, the dyslexia community uses the phrase "the science of reading" ubiquitously as a rallying cry for the education system to acknowledge the scientific evidence of how to teach struggling readers and spellers, and I agree, we need to listen to that. But this rallying cry is missing a very big piece of the puzzle. The "science of reading" often fails to include how the social and emotional health of a student can aid or prevent any intervention from being successful. Along with helping a student with reading and spelling, we need to help them understand their struggle, and they need to believe that the person helping them also truly understands dyslexia. They know right away when the person working with them does not understand. When someone says any variation of the following things to someone with dyslexia, "Try harder," "Look at the words," "Try it again," "We've been over this before," it is a red flag that they do not understand that the student is trying as hard as they can. If they could read and spell, they would, trust me.

> **The "science of reading" often fails to include how the social and emotional health of a student can aid or prevent any intervention from being successful.**

One way to accomplish this is to include time at the beginning of any intervention for conversations with each student about where they currently are and to give them a chance to describe their struggles—no matter what their age. You can't treat the reading and spelling difficulties before treating the emotional struggles and the trauma—you just can't.

Consequences of the pain

- Can lead to hesitancy to continue education.

- Creates distrust.

Students are experiencing stress-induced symptoms every day in every school, and you'd think that it would lead to some urgency in helping them. But the fact that children with dyslexia become adults with dyslexia is something that needs to be repeated over and over again. Many adults in charge of teaching kids to read (including everyone—from teachers, to parents, to teacher educators, to curriculum developers, to researchers, to administrators) underestimate the long-term effects of academic struggles and don't take into account the fact that the children internalize each and every reading and spelling failure.

> I realized it's [dyslexia] kind of brushed under the rug, but I still see that pile and know what it is. **Denisha**

 Many adults in charge of teaching kids to read underestimate the long-term effects of academic struggles and don't take into account the fact that the children internalize each and every reading and spelling failure.

What did we learn?

- The education system often does not take the extra time to acknowledge the pain and trauma that can be caused by being a student with dyslexia in the school system.
- The interventions that are chosen for struggling readers and spellers are often chosen because they are available, not because they are appropriate. These interventions need to be chosen with extreme care and expertise in order to avoid being one more thing the student cannot do.
- Students with dyslexia need to be empowered to speak up and advocate for their accommodations and be able to feel safe enough to share with the teacher that the way they are teaching is not a good fit.

Myth: They need to try harder and read more.

One thing that just about every dyslexic student will say is that they tried as hard as they could. They wanted to please their parents, their teachers, and themselves. To suggest that a child needs to try harder is to suggest that they are actively trying to not be able to read and spell at the level they are intellectually capable of. No one wants to struggle with reading, no one.

Chapter 3

Dyslexia-Induced Distrust

> My oldest is 26 and then I have a 25 and 22-year-old and I would get that feeling when I'd go to their school for appointments or meetings or conferences. And I'm adopting a 6-year-old and she's enrolling in school and I feel it again. **Josh**

Martin is a British gentleman who came to my attention a few years ago when he posted a blog about his experience with dyslexia. His piece was so full of emotion and anger about how hard it is to have dyslexia that I just couldn't stop reading it. He described his school experience this way:

> I put up with years and years of bullying, my school life was spent in the "special" class for stupid people! School was the worst experience in my life. I hear so many people say how they wish they could go back and do it again. I just think I wish I could go back and make it never happen. (Camp, 2015)

When I was lucky enough to interview him, he reiterated how his classroom struggles followed him outside of school and led to intense bullying. He was tormented by reading out loud and suggested that his dyslexia did lead him to make some poor decisions. Eventually, Martin developed a perspective that several of the adults shared:

> I've put more effort into how I deal with the backlash of being dyslexic. The biggest issue with it is other people's reactions to it. If I spell something wrong, that's not an issue. I didn't have an issue posting a message with bad spelling. It's the person that receives that message and makes a comment about it.   **Martin**

Martin is alluding to something important in that. As dyslexic children become dyslexic adults, they begin to understand that they are not stupid, lazy, or slow; they begin to realize that managing others' perceptions of people with dyslexia is the best way to deal with the lack of dyslexia awareness in the general public.

As dyslexic children become dyslexic adults, they begin to understand that they are not stupid, lazy, or slow; they begin to realize that managing others' perceptions of people with dyslexia is the best way to deal with the lack of dyslexia awareness in the general public.

Bullying and feeling shame are some of the reasons that adults are extremely reluctant to head back to a school campus for any reason. In fact, several adults who had school-aged children described having a visceral response when they had to go back into a school setting. This is an extremely important point to consider when educators are working with the parents of struggling readers. It has to be assumed that there is a significant likelihood that one of the parents also struggled. So, when the parent either disengages or engages assertively, they are coming from a place of trying to protect their child from what they experienced. They might disengage because they prefer to help their child on their own due to distrust of the system or because they are still struggling with their own literacy skills. They might become more assertive because they know what their child is capable of. Philomena described her feelings while she watched her daughter go to school on her first day:

> I found that I had panic attacks the first day she [her daughter] went out. She was happy, she was really happy about school, but I was panicking when she went in.   **Philomena**

Several adults who had school-aged children described having a visceral response when they had to go back into a school setting. This is an extremely important point to consider when educators are working with the parents of struggling readers.

Another consequence of unidentified dyslexia is making life choices that lead to feeling like some aspirations were unfilled. This unfulfillment ranges from not having children, to not going back to school, to quitting jobs, to not applying for jobs, to being extremely reluctant to share this experience with the children and grandchildren they do have. They go to great lengths to hide their dyslexia in all of these situations.

Consequences of trauma

- Intense desire to hide dyslexia.
- Decisions that lead to poor life outcomes.

Tom was an older gentleman, who met me with his wife. She joined the interview to help Tom tell his story because he was a man of few words. He rarely, if ever, talked to anyone about his dyslexia. Once he did begin to open up, with the help of his lovely wife, he revealed his anger about his dyslexia and the frustration it caused him as a child, until eventually, he just decided to stop caring about it. He spent his life doing several different jobs, all of which required little reading and more hands-on work. He was good at everything he did, but he avoided jobs that required too much writing and he never told anyone about his struggles with reading and spelling. His wife told me about their granddaughter who is also struggling in school, as well as their son who struggled through school. I asked if he had ever shared his story with his son or granddaughter; he vehemently said, "No." It never even occurred to him. I suggested that it might be nice for them to know they aren't alone, but he stood his ground—and there's nothing wrong that, it's his choice. But we have to try to understand where this need to hide and reluctance to share is coming from. I asked Tom why he hid his dyslexia, and he explained it this way:

> I just do. I don't feel like I'm dumb, so I don't bring it out. I'm pretty good at hiding stuff. I've been hiding it for 70 years. **Tom**

> **Tom was good at everything he did, but he avoided jobs that required too much writing and he never told anyone about his struggles with reading and spelling.**

More than one adult shared that they decided not to have children because they did not want to pass on their dyslexia. The adults who shared this sentiment did tend to be on the more severe side of the dyslexia continuum.

> I did not want a child to be like me. That's the reason I never had kids. **Suz**

> I believe I've never had children because I didn't want them because of my dyslexia, I didn't want to pass my blood. **Eddie**

For those who do have children, there is a level of mistrust of the educational system. Many adults expressed feeling that the school system did not take care of them, and now they do not trust that same system.

> **We have to be careful not to blame the student for not responding to the intervention. It's not the fault of the student, it's the fault of the instruction.**

I met Denisha at a coffee shop in Nebraska. She was a beautiful African American woman. She was guarded and quiet as we got comfortable while talking about the weather and my flight to Nebraska. As we settled in and I started asking my questions, Denisha became more and more vocal about how frustrated she was with her education, but the real pain became apparent when she began talking about her dyslexic son. She knew her own struggles with literacy were making it difficult, nearly impossible, for her to advocate for her son. He was being labeled as having a behavior problem but Denisha knew it was the result of dyslexia. She believed the school was taking advantage of her by not acting on her suspicion that her son was dyslexic. She felt powerless because her reading skills did not allow her to fully participate in the decision making—and it was killing her emotionally. She felt helpless and, as I listened, so did I. She needed a local advocate to go to meetings with her and help her read all the documents that were coming home from the school. She shared that when she went to meetings with the school, she believed staff took advantage of her low literacy skills and she felt completely helpless to advocate for her son. She knew how it felt to struggle with reading and spelling like he was, and she knew the school was erroneously blaming his academic problems on his behavior. Denisha felt like she was being victimized a second time—this experience is traumatic.

> **Denisha knew her own struggles with literacy were making it difficult, nearly impossible, for her to advocate for her son. He was being labeled as having a behavior problem but Denisha knew it was the result of dyslexia.**

When I met Denisha, she was trying to advocate for her son. She had been to several IEP meetings and she was adamant that he wasn't just a behavior problem. She knew his behaviors were a result of his dyslexia, not the cause. Denisha was at a disadvantage in this situation for several reasons: her own literacy skills were quite low, she was a person of color, she had limited resources, and she was a single parent. She attended school meetings alone and often felt shut down by the team. I asked her, "Why did you decide that you weren't going to let him [her son] fail?" She said, "My school failed me. And I am trying to do my best to make sure they don't fail my child. I'm going to be honest—I don't feel like I am doing good enough because it's like the more I advocate, the more they shut me down."

> **Denisha was at a disadvantage in this situation for several reasons: her own literacy skills were quite low, she was a person of color, she had limited resources, and she was a single parent. She attended school meetings alone and often felt shut down by the team.**

She later expressed that she was also too scared to go back to school to try to become a nurse.

> I wanted to be a nurse. I'm too afraid to go to school.   **Denisha**

Cary described a feeling of missed opportunity in this way:

> If younger again, I would have been more confident in pursuing the thing that I actually had a much higher aptitude for. I think I would be somewhere very different.   Cary

Will wanted to go to college but decided against it:

> I thought about it, but not really because I didn't want more stressful nights and because it was just—it was just going to be too much.   Will

For Cary and Denisha, their distrust of a system that failed them has stopped them from pursuing their own personal goals. Many of the adults expressed frustration in the lack of resources or help available for adults with dyslexia so that they can meet those goals:

> And I have said this since I was young that at some point, you gotta transition and the focus has got to be on the adult with dyslexia. It doesn't go away, it's not like when you get done with a school and they've taught you how to use a spellcheck and do this and do that. That is the very, very tip of the iceberg of functioning at a high professional level with dyslexia in the workforce. And that's my biggest frustration at this point in my life—I mean, it's going to tutorials on programs and saying anything. And it's all centered around students. It's always centered around the student that has dyslexia. Well, all the students are

becoming adults, are going into the workforce. And they're disappeared at least—at least my experience has been. And so it doesn't mean that they're not struggling. Exactly what it is that I've been looking for—that continuing professional development for adults with dyslexia and teaching them that, "Yes, you've struggled with this. This is how you talk to your employer. If you want to talk, here's the pros and cons. Here's how to deal with an email inbox when you're getting 100 emails a day. But if you spent all the time to read every email, you would be at work for 12 hours a day. Here are your organizational issues. And here are some strategies, too." And I know that those things are much more prominent in education now, teaching students with dyslexia. But having a full-time job and dealing with dyslexia is so different than getting an education with dyslexia. They're completely different worlds. **Cary**

Some people need help navigating their child's school system, some need help understanding their rights in the workplace, some need help understanding their rights in continuing education, and some expressed feeling extremely isolated and wanted a place to connect with other dyslexic adults. When they asked for connections to other adults, they were clear that they wanted those adults to be "regular," everyday people who were relatable.

Children who struggle in school never forget their school experiences. They never forget the words that were said to them about their academic struggles by the adults who were supposed to understand them. They never forget that they were left to struggle year after year by the universities that failed to adequately teach teachers about dyslexia.

A few adults mentioned that they had contemplated ending their own life and attributed this to their dyslexia. One adult, a prison inmate named Anthony, stated that:

It was either learn to read or kill myself.   **Anthony**

Another adult shared a letter his dad wrote to the district informing them that their inability to help his son had led to his son trying to take his own life. It is interesting that these two adults could not have had a more different upbringing and level of support, yet both experienced the same amount of shame and frustration. Suz was an adult who was a bit reluctant to meet with me. She spent most of her life hiding her dyslexia from peers and coworkers. Suz was a middle-aged woman, who had a good job at a big company. She spent most of her days answering customer-service questions and reading from a computer screen. She shared how exhausted she was by the end of the day. She had to spend so much cognitive energy on reading at work that when she got home she could not look at another screen or another word. Suz shared that as a child, she did not have home support or school support. She only received an intervention when she sought it out on her own as an adult and has only found one person who she believed could help her. She was simultaneously angry and very sad about situation. Her shame was so deep that she had experienced suicidal thoughts; she shared:

I wanted to end my life because it was just so bad some days. **Suz**

Like many of the adults, she was both angry about being not being identified or helped and relieved about finally being able to talk about it. At least two other adults also expressed that they had experienced suicidal thoughts due to their dyslexia.

> I did a good job of making sure that I hid [dyslexia] away and most people don't know. And when it would be pried to the forefront, that's when it became really traumatic for me. For me it was a lot of work to hide it. **Adam**

Several of the adults attributed substance abuse issues to their dyslexia. Philomena said:

> If somebody keeps telling you for 10, 15, 20 years that you're stupid, you are going to behave stupidly. **Philomena**

Earl described it this way:

> That shame and guilt and feeling less than. And I began prescribing my own medication with the whole drug and alcohol thing. I was self-medicating because of the shame and guilt, which was a consequence of dyslexia. My father was a doctor, my mom was a teacher, and I was a dummy. **Earl**

The day-to-day internal dialogue was that they were less than, and they equated dyslexia with low intelligence.

There are many aspects of school that can be traumatizing, but it is the constant day-to-day failure to meet expectations and public humiliation that cause the most harm. These are totally avoidable if the education community takes note of them. Many students who don't respond to school interventions are labeled as "poor responders." Students who don't learn to read at the same rate as their non-dyslexic peers are labeled "late bloomers." If you look at this more rationally, it is so obvious that it is the education system that is the poor responder and the late bloomer.

> **There are many aspects of school that can be traumatizing, but it is the constant day-to-day failure to meet expectations and public humiliation that cause the most harm.**

What did we learn?

- As adults enter the workplace, they often take measures to hide their dyslexia and are fearful that they will be "found out." In order to lessen this burden, dyslexia training should be part of a corporate training infrastructure, as well as part of the training for higher education and vocational training institution staff.
- Students leaving high school are unaware of their rights as they pursue higher education or vocational training programs. They need to be educated about their rights under the Americans with Disabilities Act (ADA) so they are less likely to drop out of these programs.
- Many of the adults expressed that they felt extreme sadness, depression, and frustration as a result of their school experience. For many, this could have tragic

consequences. Therefore, the mental health of those with dyslexia needs to be monitored and valued.

- Students with dyslexia feel isolated and believe they are the only one in the classroom, or even the school, who isn't "getting it." If we have mentors with dyslexia in the school, these students would have a built-in support system. This would be extremely important for those students who do not have home support or advocates.

- When an adult with dyslexia ends up incarcerated and believes it is because of their literacy struggles, it is probably true. We need to make sure the legal system and the prison system are educated about dyslexia on a large scale.

Myth: Dyslexia is a silent disability.

Dyslexia is not a silent disability. In fact, dyslexia is quite evident when dyslexics read out loud—which is not a silent activity. When they cry, it's not silent. When they act out, it's not silent. When they misspell a word for everyone to see, it's not silent.

Chapter 4

Traumatic Teaching Practices

> In English class, when it came to me to read out loud, I was like "Nah, I'm good." And the teacher proceeded to say, "Oh, come on, you can do it. I will help you." And it was pretty traumatic. I mean. I just wanted the moment to be over. I didn't want the attention drawn to me and she did the exact opposite to really showcase that, yeah, reading out loud was a major issue. And it was in front of all the students. **Cary**

Hannah is an exceptional young woman. She is articulate, independent, charming, and incredibly intelligent. When we met, she was a recent college graduate with a degree in English from a prestigious university. Hannah was assessed and identified in second grade (ages seven to eight) and from there she was able to receive tutoring using the Orton-Gillingham approach. Even though Hannah was lucky to have the education she did, she reflected on some things that still happen that can create doubt and shame:

I think that something happened that I've been thinking about a lot. Like when you're constantly being pulled out of the classroom, that is very isolating and makes you think like, "What's wrong with me?" I remember in third grade, we were standing in line, and we were all going back into the classroom. And the teacher said, "Everyone's going to go do this in the classroom, but I'm going to stay out here with someone who's very special." And then we sat. And I was like, it was me. And I was like, "Okay." And I was like, "Oh, cool, I'm special." But actually, what it was is we were sitting in the hallway and I began to read *Green Eggs and Ham*, and I couldn't do it. And it was humiliating to be like, "Okay, I'm different. I know that I should be able to read this at this grade level. I'm not dumb." **Hannah**

Orton-Gillingham is an approach to the teaching of reading and spelling that is multisensory, explicit, and systematic. It teaches the student in a small group or one-on-one setting the underlying structure of the English language.

High school was difficult because the private school she attended did not have to give her accommodations, and they often withheld these from her. By the time she was a senior in high school, she was a disability activist and she spent time listening to other dyslexics talk about their experiences. This led her to finally be able to ask her teachers not to make her read out loud, which she said did not go well. She did express that it would have been nice to have someone at the school who understood dyslexia:

> So I think that, to have someone who genuinely understood and was equally fighting for me would've been great. **Hannah**

When we spoke, she was working in the film production industry and had decided that she would not reveal that she is dyslexic to her boss. She did not believe that her boss would understand dyslexia and thought they might perceive it as a weakness or an excuse. Hannah continues to learn how to advocate for others and will be that person she wished she'd had in high school.

> My schooling years were fairly traumatic and extremely awful, really awful. **Philomena**

> **Every adult I interviewed expressed that the single most traumatizing thing they had had to do was read out loud.**

Every adult I interviewed expressed that the single most traumatizing thing they had had to do was read out loud in many different situations. The experiences of reading out loud happened in classrooms and in other public spaces, like church. The adults could describe the experience of reading out loud in public as if it happened yesterday, which means that it is something they will likely not forget. I asked each adult to use one word to describe reading out loud, and almost every time, their eyes would fill with tears as if they were reliving the moment. They would look down or away and they would often apologize for their emotional response. The memories and attached emotions still hurt, decades later. Their body language spoke volumes about the impact of teaching practices like round robin reading, popcorn reading, and peer reading, which don't have research to back up the validity of their use (Hilden & Jones, 2012; Ortiz & Rasinski, 2008).

I asked each adult to use one word to describe reading out loud, and almost every time, their eyes would fill with tears as if they were reliving the moment. They would look down or away and they would often apologize for their emotional response.

In round-robin reading, the class reads the same text while students are randomly called on to read out loud.

In popcorn reading, the class is reading the same text and when a student completes their section out loud, they randomly choose the next reader.

In peer reading, students are paired with another student and they read to each other.

Their body language spoke volumes about the impact of teaching practices like round robin reading, popcorn reading, and peer reading.

But the words they chose when answering my question came

easily, and even if they used different words, they all carried the same connotation of trauma. Keep in mind that what the adults share below about reading out loud is not a single incident. They had to experience it every single time they went to school. These experiences happen on a daily basis and are prolonged over years:

[When reading out loud] you get the feeling—I always associate with this tingly, hot, sweaty feeling on the back of my neck. Like everyone's staring at you, and the eyeballs are digging in and you just freak out. My heart would race. I still get that feeling. **Josh**

Embarrassing. Like you don't know how. It was just a torment to me. **Charles**

It was terrifying, and I would cry. I remember crying sometimes because the teacher was not very nice—this was my first-grade teacher. She would sort of make fun of me, so it was terrifying. **Beth**

Scared and just like, angry. I wanted to run away from them. **Adam**

That [reading out loud] was absolutely terrifying. Traumatizing. Because it was like terrible in the moment. But then it was also terrible after, when I was rethinking it. It was more what everyone was thinking of me and just having it in my head that everyone thinks I am stupid kind of thing. **Tannis**

I want to say it's [reading out loud] I can only imagine it's what having an asthma attack would feel like. Panicky. I was thinking—Oh, they are going to call me on soon, I have to make sure—look for words you're going to pronounce wrong. Because you don't want to be the kid who goes too slow and everybody's like, "Would they just finish?" But you also don't want to rush things and mess them up. **Kendall**

I'm just fearing that the world is going to cave in on me when it [reading out loud] gets to me. **Angela**

Torment. **Charles**

We were at the Smithsonian one time and there was a wall text describing the exhibit. My dad wanted me to stand there and read the wall text...it took me about 15 minutes to get through and it was just so embarrassing. **Riley**

That was absolutely terrifying. I had many strategies to get around that. **Cary**

What you do, what you say, and not say greatly impacts a student for their entire life. When you publicly shame a student for spelling a word wrong, or reading a word wrong matters. **Amy T.**

> I sat in a professional development two months ago where our reading coach randomly starting picking on people to read from the...board, and I was like, no, scanning the words to make sure I knew them because if she called on me I needed to be ready. And I was really thankful she didn't call on me. There is a physical reaction that happens when you feel like you could be called on. **Angela**

> In high school I had a teacher who was going to help me. When I was there, I had to stand by her desk and read, and she had brought out a first-grade reading book out [sic]. Well, that's a goddamn bad, bad mistake. **Tom**

Students with dyslexia should only read out loud if they volunteer and/or if they are in a safe one-on-one situation.

Students with dyslexia should only read out loud if they volunteer and/or if they are in a safe one-on-one situation. Being subjected to teaching practices like reading out loud in front of peers leads to long-term consequences for students. In fact, anything that highlights a student's shortcomings due to dyslexia in front of their peers should be avoided. This includes peer-grading, spelling bees, posting unedited writing on the wall, etc. Yes, students with dyslexia want to do well and they want their work on the wall with everyone else, but only if they approve it. Peers should never grade a dyslexic's spelling test, or any test for that matter.

Anything that highlights a student's shortcomings due to dyslexia in front of their peers should be avoided.

It's imperative to remember that every adult I interviewed was bright and articulate. When they were behind their peers, they knew it, and because of their intellect, not understanding why their peers understood something (reading and spelling) and they didn't was extremely frustrating. When peers notice this it can lead to bullying and isolation.

Consequences of traumatic teaching practices

- They can lead to bullying.

- They can lead to a distrust of the education system.

- They can lead to physical symptoms.

Students with dyslexia want to do well and they want their work on the wall with everyone else, but only if they approve it. Peers should never grade a dyslexic's spelling test, or any test for that matter.

School can be traumatizing for a lot of people for a lot of different reasons, and just about everyone can come up with an embarrassing event that happened during their K-12 (kindergarten to twelfth grade) career. But most people didn't experience the daily trauma that many kids with dyslexia do. In fact, just waking up knowing they have to go to school every day and struggle with reading and spelling is traumatizing. Josh described what it is like to go into a situation every single day and know that no one there understands how to help you, with this brilliant analogy.

> I've used this analogy before trying to explain it [trauma] to people. If you can't swim in our society, you're not dysaquatic. You just can't swim, and there's no word for it. Nobody says, "Wow"—they might say, "Wow, you can't swim? That's weird. Okay, we won't go to the pool." And that's basically the end of it. Or, if you're going on a boat, wear a life jacket. But if you can't read or you can't spell then something's wrong with you. And if you think about it further, pools are designed for people who can't swim because there is a shallow end. They can still go to the pool, but they don't go in the deep end.   **Josh**

> **Just waking up knowing they have to go to school every day and struggle with reading and spelling is traumatizing.**

When it comes to consistent themes across stories, trauma was the most common. In fact, what the adults shared was consistent with what Dr. Neil Alexander-Passe (2018) found when he studied adult dyslexics. His research suggests that it is very likely that students with dyslexia who are not identified and who do not receive the instruction and care that they require show symptoms of Post-Traumatic Stress Disorder (PTSD). Using the DSM-IV (the *Diagnostic and Statistical Manual of Mental Disorders, fourth edition*) definition of PTSD, he found that trauma in dyslexics can be caused by various situations, including: the sudden exclusion from their peer group; intense anger from a teacher or parent; physical bullying at school; a realization that something unrecognizable is wrong.

Stacey summed it up this way:

> I have been riddled with anxiety, frequently feeling inadequate and deficient. **Stacey**

Neil Alexander-Passe found that trauma in dyslexics can be caused by various situations, including: the sudden exclusion from their peer group; intense anger from a teacher or parent; physical bullying at school; a realization that something unrecognizable is wrong.

Accommodations are tools that students can use to help them access information in an alternate format. They allow the student to access information at their intellectual level rather than their reading level. They range from providing more time on tests and assignments to using assistive technology (see 'Acknowledge, Advocate, and Accommodate' for more information). Accommodations should play a significant role in a dyslexic's life. They should be offered in kindergarten and be available throughout life.

Accommodations should play a significant role in a dyslexic's life.

Accommodations are not an unfair advantage; in fact, they could be the one thing that determines if someone succeeds or not. They might determine how someone views their own self-worth. They give a dyslexic student the ability to showcase their true intellectual capability. Hannah shared that when she was in a private school, the school refused to give her extra time to complete an exam and talked about how that impacted her:

> It was a very traumatic experience because I did not finish a test almost my entire high school experience.   **Hannah**

 Accommodations give a dyslexic student the ability to showcase their true intellectual capability.

What did we learn?

- Most of the adults with dyslexia believed that none of their teachers had understood their experience. If every educator, at every level, was required to participate in a dyslexia simulation to understand the emotional and social impact of some teaching practices on struggling students, this might decrease the isolation these students feel. The Dyslexia for a Day simulation (see the Resources section) is a way to accomplish this goal.

- Students with dyslexia should be knowledgeable about their rights under IDEA that protect them from teaching practices, like reading out loud, and how to advocate for them. The IDEA (Individuals with Disabilities Education Act) was originally created to give school-age children with disabilities the opportunity to access a free public education. Since its inception it has been improved and edited, and parents and students should be knowledgeable about their rights under Individuals with Disabilities Education Act (IDEA) that protect them from denial or delay of an appropriate education. IDEA also includes protections to make sure the student is identified for services at the school that are individualized to the student and describes instruction that is appropriate and provides accommodations.

Myth: **They just haven't found a book they like yet.**

Trust me when I say: if a child who is struggling could read, they would.

Chapter 5

Is Spelling Important to You?

> At around the age of 50, I was asked by the principal (she was a teacher) to come to the board and write some of our ideas for a meeting we were having. I could not spell some of the words and felt terrible. **Melissa**

One morning, I found myself at an IEP meeting as an advocate for a boy of around 12 years old named Eric. I was sitting at a table with his mom and six or seven other members of the team, who represented the school. As we began talking about goals and what he would learn during the next 12 months, the topic of spelling came up. We tussled a little and went back and forth about why we should or should not be teaching Eric to spell. The school team shared that they did not think spelling was important, "especially with all the technology and spellcheck." My experience of working with adults told me otherwise. I knew they were embarrassed by their spelling, and I knew their spelling held them back. I also knew that spellcheck doesn't catch many mistakes. More than one adult expressed that they "could beat spellcheck." After observing and listening to adults with dyslexia, I know that telling a student not to worry about spelling while writing doesn't work. They will still choose to use the word "big" instead of "enormous," even though they want to use the more sophisticated word. I know they are humiliated when those writing samples go up on the wall for back-to-school night. So, as I sat and listened to the reasoning of why he didn't need to be taught spelling, it dawned on me that everyone at that table could spell. This is an important observation. What was really going was an unconscious effort to marginalize a student. The real problem was that they didn't know how to teach spelling, so they decided it was okay if some of their students were only partially literate. I wondered if anyone had ever asked Eric if he wanted to learn to spell. I wondered if they had ever considered what kind of impact poor spelling might actually have on his life as an adult when he was no longer protected by special education law, provided with accommodations, and protected by his parents.

This brings me to the question that several of the adults asked me: Why aren't more dyslexics at the table when these decisions are made?

One of my first interviewees, Sean, shared that he was frustrated by the lack of representation of dyslexics in meetings and conferences that are about people with dyslexia. He was airing a common frustration among dyslexic adults that there are not enough dyslexics at the table to share their experience and their ideas about how to help—

and the point is extremely valid. I didn't know how to answer the question and I still don't. But I think that we have to invite them, and we have to make sure that when they do voice their opinions, we don't silence them. Their opinions might go against the science and research to which we are so beholden, and if they do, we should think seriously about that but not without the voices of those with dyslexia. Think about how difficult it might be to join the conversation and add your voice when you are dyslexic and the world is so text heavy. People with dyslexia need to educate us about how they were able to become successful.

When it comes to spelling, I asked all the dyslexic adults: Is spelling important and if so, has it ever affected you negatively or caused embarrassment? Without hesitation, the answer was a resounding, "Yes and yes!"

Teaching someone to read is important; this is something that everyone can agree on. But when it comes to the importance of teaching spelling, it seems we haven't asked those with dyslexia if they think it's important. But I did. When it comes to spelling, I asked them all: Is spelling important and if so, has it ever affected you negatively or caused embarrassment? Without hesitation, the answer was a resounding, "Yes and yes!":

I still get embarrassed when I cannot spell a simple word. Mainly because there is a stigma that if you can't spell you are not intelligent.   **Anonymous**

I spend a great deal of time with spellcheck. And I often cannot even get close enough to have spellcheckers get the right word so sometimes I have to use a different word which can change the meaning or effect of the sentence. I very much wish I was a better speller.   **Bob**

If I was a better speller all of my dreams would have came true in life like being married, having children, and having a life.   **Eddie**

I always beat myself up. Sometimes I would get the words right but when the dreaded spelling test would come up it was like stabbing pain in my back. It was the worst pain and suffering I ever went through. It was horrible. It was really horrible.   **Adam**

I do think people need to know how to spell. I might be taking notes somewhere and someone looks over at my notes, I'll know what it meant, but they'd be like "Whoa."   **Beth**

Horrible. It just like—I mean honestly, it makes me feel really stupid and it makes me so frustrated to this day.   **Peggy**

On a professional level, it [spelling] is the main reason why I am not in my degree field of work. Everyone always tells me well there is spellcheck and why are you here (in a factory) with a degree. I always tell them that spellcheck really isn't usefully for me. Either because it has no idea what am I trying to spell or I do not know the correct spelling or just the way it sounds. **Natalee**

Yes, I just didn't write or communicate or didn't try to spell something. I just kept it to myself, I didn't want to be embarrassed. **Riley**

It [spelling] has made me very self-conscious, it has made me avoid certain situations, it has made me feel like I'm a loser because I couldn't spell when I was younger. **Anonymous**

Although this is just a sample of the answers I received, at least 47 of the 50+ adults were adamant that spelling was important, that it was hard, and that it has caused embarrassment at some point. For some, it impeded their ability to move forward at work, and for others, it made it difficult to jot down an impromptu grocery list.

It is not as if they are not acutely aware of their reading and spelling struggles very early on; they are. We can't sweep spelling struggles under the rug with accommodations; instead, we have to tackle them head on. But in order to do that, we have to make sure those who are teaching the students who are hardest to teach are highly trained. In order to gain the trust of the struggling students, we have to prove to them that we know what we are doing—that is really the half the battle. Remember, as dyslexic students have got older and moved through the system, they have come in contact with educators who have tried to help them, but if they were not skilled, it didn't work. Each one of those instructional failures was internalized by the students as their failure. The teacher who can make the most significant impact is one who proves they understand dyslexia and how to teach a struggling student; otherwise, we will be just another teacher in a long line of teachers who can't help—and that is devastatingly frustrating to dyslexics.

What did we learn?

- Educators who can spell should not determine that students do not need to learn this skill. The adults in this book with dyslexia shared how spelling has affected them, and their stories should impact how the curriculum is created and spelling is approached.

Myth: **Spelling doesn't matter.**

It matters. It matters to anyone who has ever been made fun of because of their spelling. It matters to anyone who didn't apply for a job or a promotion because of their spelling. It matters to those who have their writing pinned to the classroom wall. It matters when a person is forced to use a smaller word when they are intellectually capable of a more complex word. It matters.

Chapter 6

Do You Think Dyslexia Is a Gift?

Anthony was an inmate who believed he was incarcerated for most of life because of his lack of literacy skills. When I asked him if he thought dyslexia was a gift, he literally laughed, looked around at his surroundings (a California prison) and said, "Definitely not."

This question about dyslexia being a gift is a tricky one and one that needs to be parsed out. First, let's talk about what a gift is. The word gift has a few meanings. The *Oxford Dictionary of English* says it can mean: *a thing given willingly to someone without payment; a present,* as in "I bought a gift for my teacher." It can also mean: *a natural ability or talent,* as in "That girl had a gift for drawing." It can also be a verb: (gift someone with): *endow with (something),* as in "He was gifted with the ability of public speaking." The connotation of a gift, when studied in context, is positive. So, when we refer to dyslexia as a gift and then list famous dyslexic people, we may be appealing to some people while alienating others. If we use the definitions above, our message is that you have received something innately wonderful. But that is not how those with dyslexia describe it. Those who do believe it has been a positive force in their lives state that dyslexia is a gift because it forces you to work harder, to find workarounds, and to improve other skills that do not require intense written skills. The adults in these interviews did not think it was a gift when they were children and could only see its benefits in retrospect. In fact, most agreed that saying that dyslexia is a wonderful gift might be a slap in the face to the kid who is struggling every single day and who really has no power to change their situation.

> **The adults in these interviews did not think dyslexia was a gift when they were children and could only see its benefits in retrospect.**

Instead, I offer that dyslexia is a hurdle. A hurdle is *an obstacle or difficulty*. Hurdles are meant to be cleared. Usually, when we clear a hurdle, we learn something and we become stronger. We are able to clear hurdles with lots of support, training, and effort. When we don't clear hurdles, we are stuck, or we feel like failures. Dyslexia is a hurdle, not a gift. Most of the adults interviewed for this book described dyslexia as an awful part of their childhood. Only those who were able to clear the hurdle and accomplish their goals could look back and see dyslexia as a positive force in their lives. Those adults generally had home and school support. The adults without that support were almost offended by the idea that dyslexia could be a positive force in their lives:

Peggy, who works with dyslexic kids shared:

...kids feel that pressure. I mean because I work with all the kids and all of them say, "If one more person tells me that Einstein was dyslexic, I'm going to scream." I mean it doesn't help them. **Peggy**

All the adults were asked if they thought dyslexia was a gift. With the exception of a very small handful of adults, they all said no. They explained this in the following ways:

I have been telling my children that since the time they were diagnosed. It's not a gift. It's a handicap. It's not easy to survive with it. But when you tell children that—I always told my kids, the only people who have this are smart, brilliant people, and they're—which is probably true, but not a gift. It's hard, bloody work. **Philomena**

Sometimes when I read, I can't get to the end of the paragraph because I have to really dissect each word, each sentence to get to an understanding of their meaning. But I did get a good base understanding and I zoomed through from that point. So would I give that away? No, because that part was a gift, even though it had consequences. You might not see it was a gift. Is it a gift or a curse? **Earl**

What is it giving me? It's not giving me anything. It's holding me back from a lot of things. So how is that a gift? **Suz**

It's only a gift if you can survive it. **Lois**

Dyslexia is interesting because you live in this crazy dichotomy where most teachers think you are stupid, but a few teachers think you are brilliant. Sometimes you know you are brilliant, until your brain fails you, and reminds you that you can't do basic tasks that your peers can do with minimal effort. Dyslexia is my kryptonite. **Amy T.**

Some days I wonder why things couldn't just be normal. But on the other hand, it's like if I weren't dyslexic I wouldn't have had some of the struggles I did and I wouldn't have advocated the way that I have. I truly think it's a gift depending on how you embrace it. **Nicole**

I don't think dyslexia is a gift but you just deal with what you got. **Riley**

Absolutely NOT, I hate that comment. Any kind of struggle affects people differently. It can have a good effect, build up your stamina to keep trying to learn, it makes you develop different coping skills but that is all a result of the struggle to overcome a difficulty with reading. It also could have a very negative effect. Low self-esteem, giving up easily, not reading or writing well. Not getting to your full potential. It's absolutely not a gift. **Beth**

Nah, no, I think we are defined by our struggles and we're not defined by things that are easy. **Tim**

> Dyslexia sure didn't feel like a gift growing up. Some days it still doesn't feel like a gift. I think all our life experiences help mold us into who we are but to say dyslexia is a gift feels like a longshot. I am, however, very reluctant to take away any magic that might be in the statement. **Stacey**

> If you ask a dyslexic, they're not going to say it's a gift. I don't think so, because the...words that come to mind are frustrating, my biggest one, embarrassment—I personally don't think of it as gift as a kid. There is no gift. I have to work extremely hard. **Angela**

> It's a nightmare. **Tom**

Of course, there is a lot of good that can come from finding positive role models in the dyslexia community and using their success as a beacon of hope for young kids who are struggling. But we need to be responsible with that message and make sure we are finding relatable heroes who look, sound, and live like the adults I interviewed.

What did we learn?

- It is almost offensive to tell a struggling kid they are lucky. It is nice to have role models, but those role models must reflect the demographics of all students. Adults with dyslexia, from all walks of life, need to be more vocal about the messages that are pervasive in the dyslexic community. They need to feel more comfortable in correcting myths about dyslexia.

- The voices in the dyslexia community need to be more diversified in terms of success, socio-economic status, ethnicity, and perspective.
- Adults with dyslexia would benefit from a community where they can share ideas about how to succeed at work and school.

Myth: (kind of): Dyslexia is a gift.

The real answer is—it's a hurdle. Hurdles are meant to be cleared with a lot of hard work and determination. Hurdles are smaller for students with more support than they are for other students. That hard word and determination leads to getting better and better at what you are doing. That could be music, art, public speaking, tennis, etc. Hurdles might also steer us in a new direction. Some adults with dyslexia thought they were successful because they were forced to do things that didn't have to do with language. While hurdles are not innate gifts, they are gifts in that they can foster resilience.

Chapter 7

Has Dyslexia Affected Your Ability to Succeed?

> You're disenfranchising a person when you take away their right to learn the same as another person. More long term, you take away their agency of being understood.   Tim

> **Adam was able to go to college to play football, but this is where he really paid the price for his dyslexia. He was relegated to the bleachers while he watched his own football team play without him; he was not allowed to play due to his grades.**

Adam was one of my first interviews. He was a little nervous and not used to telling his story. He is a stay-at-home dad to two small children and is a part-time park ranger. Adam described his school experience as an exercise in trying to figure out what was "wrong" with him. Adam's mom and stepdad were a significant source of support for Adam. Adam was finally diagnosed when he was a teenager. He received some support in high school, but he really credits his superior athletic ability with saving his high-school career. He was able to go to college to play football, but this is where he really paid the price for his dyslexia. He was relegated to the bleachers while he watched his own football team play without him; he was not allowed to play due to his grades. While he told this story he held back tears; this was clearly traumatic. But the trauma wasn't isolated to school. Adam relayed stories of being humiliated about his spelling at work, in front of coworkers. He recounted a particular story of a supervisor taking something that Adam had written, printing it out, and showing it to the staff. And then this happened:

I had some part-time jobs. And one of them was, I was a trip coordinator and I did trips for the military and civilians. And I coordinated all the bus trips to Niagara Falls or to New York. And it was a lot of written correspondence because you have [inaudible] the bus lines and make flyers... But anyway, I had a boss, the supervisor said, "Read this email now that you sent." Yeah. Okay. "Now read it out loud." Just very abrupt, and they knew I had dyslexia. And I remember she said to me, in front—and this is in the office in front of everyone else, the two other people that I've worked with. She's basically getting very, very loud with me and I said, "Okay," and she goes, "You don't see it. Do you?" I said, "See what?" You spelled sing instead of sign. And I'm like, okay. She said, "You should make a list of words that you misspell commonly." And I said, "That's the dictionary." And she looked at me and she got mad at me. "You need to be professional." And I said to her, I said, "Did you ever make somebody get out of a wheelchair and tell them to walk when they couldn't?" And I said, "You can't just do that." And it took a lot of strength, and just, a long story short, I had a talk with my wife, and I'm not one of those people that complain a lot about stuff because throughout my life I've been beat down like that, but that part just—I'm a man and she just belittled me in front of my coworkers and just was nasty. So I thought, "You know what? That's enough of that. I don't need to be treated that way." And then I resigned and I found a better job.   **Adam**

That is a traumatic event. That is an event that can keep someone from going back to school, from pursuing job opportunities, and from ever writing again. It is also evidence that we have a long way to go in educating the public, the workforce, corporations, and the those who work within the legal system about how dyslexia affects adults at work and at home. Adam was very interested in understanding what his legal rights were in the workplace, and rightly so. Adam was so honest and open. He was so interested in making sure his story helped someone else who has dyslexia. He was so smart and kind. He was traumatized by his school experience, but his home support and the resources his parents had were surely a major reason he was able to successfully navigate adulthood. Adam had the unrelenting support of his mom and she advocated for him throughout his school years. His stepdad was able to have him assessed, and the subsequent diagnosis provided him with the answers he needed about why Adam was struggling and how to help him.

We have a long way to go in educating the public, the workforce, corporations, and the those who work within the legal system about how dyslexia affects adults at work and at home.

> Put it this way...you can never relax. Life is a constant struggle for most basic things that other people get to take for granted. **Peggy**

Many of the adults were very interested in whether or not they were protected by disability laws. They were also frustrated that once they graduated from high school, it seemed that all of the support and guidance disappeared. They believed that if they revealed their dyslexia to their employers, they would lose their jobs. There is a substantial need in the corporate world, higher education, and the legal system for more dyslexia awareness and disability rights education.

> **The dyslexic adults I interviewed believed that if they revealed their dyslexia to their employers, they would lose their jobs. There is a substantial need in the corporate world, higher education, and the legal system for more dyslexia awareness and disability rights education.**

When I met Gwen, a sweet, gentle soul, she was frustrated about recently dropping out of a class and felt like she was letting people down. She expressed reluctance to go back to school because was certain the teachers would not understand her. She wanted to complete her GED[1] and attend culinary school. She had attempted to do both but ultimately ended up quitting because of embarrassment.

---

1   The completion of the GED (General Educational Development Test) allows a person to enter the workforce and attend higher education even if they did not complete the traditional high school classes.

> I just feel embarrassed to even ask for the help to say, "I can't read this." Some people will be like, "You can't read that?" I'll be like, "No." "But why? Why can't you read that?" It's just like you know what, forget it, I don't need to explain that and I walk out.   **Gwen**

Most of the adults with dyslexia reported going to great lengths to hide their dyslexia from family members, teachers, and employers. They often believe that people will think they are stupid, they are not worthy, of the job or they will fail. The feelings they shared are often referred to as Imposter Syndrome. They have self-doubt about their abilities and are terrified of being "found out," which both serve to hold them back from accomplishing their goals.

> I lost my job and my friends.   **Beth**

> There were times I thought, "Well, I'm never going to get married because I can't get close to anyone because then they're going to know how stupid I am, and they're going to know. They're going to know. Someone's going to find out. You know. It's just the hiding."   **Christa**

On the flip side, there are adults who have managed to understand that it is the people who choose not to understand them who are at fault, so they no longer worry about what others think about their dyslexia. Although this can be liberating, it is often described in an angry and resentful tone, which hints that they do care and are a bit wounded.

Keeping up at work was also a major concern of many of the adults. Josh summed it up brilliantly:

> How it affects me on a day-to-day basis more or less is I can't keep up with the amount of material that I have to read. I get well over 100 emails a day and those are not in total. I get more than that, but I have filters set up to throw some of them away right away or file them where I don't have to look at them. And then I have to respond, so read the email, read the attachment, and respond to it. And by the time I open it and read it, there's already three or four more from other people with feedback and stuff. And so, I have this cumulative effect of always being behind. **Josh**

Parents' role

There are positive outcomes for many students with dyslexia. But those outcomes are not often a result of the school system; they are a result of hard work, perseverance, intelligence, grit, and advocacy. The most positive outcomes can be qualitatively correlated to home support and resources. Those without that extra support do not fare as well—they are casualties of a lack of awareness and training—unacceptable casualties.

To find out a bit about parents' perspectives on their relationships with the education system while their children were struggling, I asked some parents of the adults interviewed if the school contacted them about their children's struggles or if they had to contact the school.

We talked about this in conferences. But I finally had a heart-to-heart talk with his third-grade teacher and she asked the school personnel to contact me about him. **Parent**

The school did not approach us. We (Kendall's mother mostly) were always at the forefront pushing the school to teach to her needs. The school was not forthcoming with this information, and as we were young parents and she was our first child, we were unaware of what was available. I think parents need to be advocates for their children, because they cannot advocate for themselves in the early years. Parents need to be so careful about what teachers their child gets. It's important to have teachers who can work with not just the child, but the parents too. This can set them up for success or failure as they get older or whether or not they view their schooling in a positive way. I know this is not a question, but perhaps you can create one out of this. **Parent**

As a parent with kids with dyslexia it was hard fighting the school system to get the help they needed. I was told that dyslexia is not considered a learning disability to get funding for. I wish now I had access to more resources to help her. Luckily, there were a couple of teachers that helped me get some help but I still hit walls throughout her school years. More because teachers did not want to be bothered with the accommodations. **Parent**

> I can't think of what I would have said differently. I just wished I had insisted that the school, Adam's father, and his physician had taken my concerns more seriously and helped me through those problems. I am sad that I was so accepting of thinking others knew more about my own son than I did. **Parent**

In addition to these statements, the parents all commented on the resilience of their children and their ability to succeed. This resilience may be a direct result of parental support and advocacy. However, even their best efforts often did not result in services that were enough for their children. The most important takeaway is that the parents had to contact the school. They had to be the squeaky wheel. This is still the case today. Sadly, there are many adults who were interviewed who did not have this type of parental advocacy and many of them were not as resilient. These statements are really just confirmation of what we already know: students with advocates and involved and empowered parents are far more likely to be able to navigate adulthood successfully, but we leave the others behind and fail to acknowledge their dyslexia as being real or their motivation and effort as being enough. In the absence of adult advocacy, students need to be taught how to self-advocate.

Parents commented on the resilience of their children and their ability to succeed. This resilience may be a direct result of parental support and advocacy. However, even their best efforts often did not result in services that were enough for their children.

The idea that teachers do not reach out to parents when a child is struggling with reading and spelling is not new, but it needs to be addressed. Hannah knew what was going on when she was in school. She understood that those teaching her had an unspoken allegiance to the system, and not to her. She knew she was on her own and she knew she had to self-advocate. Kids know these things even if they cannot articulate them as well as Hannah can:

> And everyone feels so beholden to the system, that it was wrong for me to advocate for myself or to say why this is bad and try to push back because it puts them in a compromised position. So, I think that, to have someone who genuinely understood and was equally fighting for me would've been great. **Hannah**

What did we learn?

- Students who don't have advocates or involved parents will not fare as well as those who do. Without outside involvement, most of the students would never be identified—that is a tragedy and maybe even a civil rights issue. When parents cannot be the advocate, there has to be advocacy from someone within the education system. It cannot remain the case that only those with parents who are able to advocate get the help they need.
- Adults need a community. They often feel like they have been left twisting in the wind after leaving the K-12 (kindergarten to twelfth grade) system. They have much to share and they need that network to lessen the isolation. Adults with dyslexia should form a coalition

to help provide younger students with the tools and confidence they need to self-advocate.

Myth: **People outgrow their dyslexia.**

Nope. Those who don't learn to read and spell in childhood will not be able to read and spell in adulthood.

Chapter 8

Acknowledge, Advocate, and Accommodate

> The biggest problem is other people's reaction to it.
> Martin

At the beginning of each interview, I explained that I was collecting the stories of adults with dyslexia because I believed they could teach us an extraordinary amount about how to help kids who are currently struggling in school, their parents, and educators. I made a promise that the time they took to talk to me and the trust they gave to me would result in something helpful. I promised them that their stories would matter. So, now that we have taken the journey through the complicated, emotional, intelligent perspective of adult dyslexics, it is time to address what we can do to help.

Consequences of the definition dilemma

Instructions given to dyslexics might not take their emotions into account.

Research does not take the impact of emotion and trauma on testing results into account.

What can parents do?

- *Ask questions.* Ask each and every professional working with your child how they define dyslexia. Ask about the chosen intervention. How does it help? How do they know it will help? How many students with dyslexia have been successful in using the proposed intervention? Do not allow an intervention to be used that is not appropriate. What about accommodations? What do you understand about the social/emotional effects of dyslexia? Each and every question holds the school accountable for making sure what they choose causes no preventable harm. Adults report that they knew as kids when the intervention wasn't working, and this breeds frustration and anger.

- *Ask every school team: Why do you think the student is struggling with reading and spelling? Why did you wait so long?* You want an answer that is not based on test scores; you want to find out if there is a bias in the classroom. Does the teacher already think the student will always be behind? These questions can uncover bias about whether or not the school is blaming the student and/or the parent and how well they understand dyslexia. The answer will help you understand how to proceed. Do you need to educate the staff? Do you need to hire an advocate? Are they already assuming your student is expendable and maybe even unteachable?

- *Do not wait.* Red flags for dyslexia can be screened for in kindergarten. Dyslexia is not something that is outgrown. Dyslexics are not late bloomers or unmotivated. They are not reluctant readers. They don't need another year of first or second grade (ages six to eight). Every year a child goes without identification and appropriate remediation is another year they feel as though they are failing. The adults in this book shared that every time they did not respond to intervention or "extra help," they internalized that failure as being their fault. Every year that passes is more time to internalize school failures and self-blame, and the shame grows. Their anxiety increases. These children who are struggling in school never forget their school experiences. They never forget the words about their academic struggles that were said to them by the adults who were supposed to understand them. They never forget that they were left to struggle, year after year. These kids become adults who remember school as an experience they survived—but not unscathed.

> Every year that passes is more time for dyslexic children to internalize school failures and self-blame, and the shame grows. Their anxiety increases. These children who are struggling in school never forget their school experiences. They never forget the words about their academic struggles that were said to them by the adults who were supposed to understand them.

Adults with dyslexia—what can you do?

- *Take your place at the table.* Your story is the most important information we have about dyslexia. Your experiences and your advice about helping those like you is what the education community needs to really improve the current situation. Talk to a local legislator about the issues you faced as a child and the issues you face as an adult, and see what you can change.

- *Share your story as often as possible.* By sharing your story, you may be the person who provides someone else with the hope and dignity they have been looking for. Many adults shared that they go to great lengths to hide their dyslexia, but if you can muster the courage to tell your story publicly, you could be a beacon of light for someone who is still hiding.

- *Create an adult support group.* So many adults said they felt isolated and were looking for other adults to talk with. They want to talk about work-related issues, relationship issues, and all kinds of things that affect dyslexic adults. A group for adults with dyslexia to get together and share resources and ideas might lessen the isolation.

- *Don't be afraid or ashamed to ask for help.* If you are still struggling with literacy issues and want to improve them, you can reach out to organizations like ProLiteracy and public libraries to find adult-centered literacy services.

- *Talk to the local school board.* You can attend local school board meeting and share your story. Tell them about ways they can improve the lives of those currently struggling in their district.

What can we ask educators to do?

- *Advocate for preservice teaching programs to provide information about dyslexic students so that you can be that safe learning space for the students who struggle.* It's not the teachers' fault that they are not adequately trained; the blame rests on the shoulders of the universities who teach them.

- *Acknowledge the experience, the effort, and the pain, and speak their language.* When a struggling student sits down with a teacher, they already know they are struggling. They know their peers are getting something that seems elusive to them. Many have already labeled themselves as stupid or "retarded." So, before any intervention can begin, the student has to feel as though they have been heard—and understood. There has to be a conversation (a conversation, not a lecture) about what will be taught and why it will be taught. Dyslexia needs to be explained so that the student knows it is neurobiological and not something they are doing wrong or a lack of effort. Students need to be asked what they are struggling to understand, what is frustrating, and what it is they want to improve. They need to be asked what works and what doesn't. They have to be included as partners in this process and their voice is the most important voice in the process. Struggling students know when a teacher understands them; if they do not perceive that they have empathy and understanding, there will be no trust, and learning will be slow and laborious.

- *Be careful with your words and actions towards a dyslexic student.* Josh described how careless interactions have lifelong consequences:

> Don't dismiss it. It's a real thing and be careful what you say and be careful of the way you act. I think those are the things—it depends on the age, too, how you deal with a very young child is very different from an older one. I remember it was in high school, and I got laughed at by a geometry teacher or trigonometry or something like that. And I asked a question and everybody laughed. The teacher laughed. And I was like, "What the hell?" So, I dropped the class. **Josh**

- *Do not punish a student who is struggling by keeping them in at recess or after school.* Remember, a dyslexic student is trying as hard as they can and their only bright spot during the day might be lunch and recess. Punishing them for something they cannot control only works to erode their trust in your and future teachers.
- *Develop empathy.* The best way to do this is to participate in a dyslexia simulation. Simulations give the participants the opportunity to feel the anxiety and stress of having dyslexia in a classroom setting. One simulation that can accomplish this is Dyslexia for a Day (see the Resources section).
- *Employ dyslexia mentors.* Students need someone they can go to in school who understands dyslexia, but also, more importantly, understands each student's dyslexia and can help them advocate for themselves in school. Mentors are not instructors but are emotional and

social support; this will be imperative for students who are at risk for dropping out or do not have parents as advocates.

- *Make sure that adult basic educators, adult literacy tutors, and prison educators are well trained in dyslexia.* If an adult comes to a teacher in this setting, they may be their last hope. My observation in the prison was that the teachers were beyond dedicated and talented educators, but they lacked training in dyslexia.

- *Identify early, provide appropriate intervention, and never underestimate the importance of accommodations.* It can't be repeated enough: waiting is one of the most detrimental things we can do. Using interventions that are not going to work for a dyslexic student is detrimental. Denying accommodations is really denying access to an education. Katie offered this advice to teachers from the perspective of her ten-year-old self:

> Get me tested. Get me help. And you know I know the material, just give me another way to take the test or give me the hope that I need to gain the skills I can to pass the test. **Katie**

What can we ask researchers to do?

- *Conduct more qualitative research.* This book is based on qualitative-research interviews, which were then transcribed and combed through to identify common themes that were shared by the adults interviewed for the book. It's painstaking work, but it is the only way to humanize dyslexia. There are hundreds of quantitative articles about phonemic/phonological awareness, fluency, reading comprehension, etc. With this information, the term "Science of Reading" has been coined and used as evidence for how to teach reading. But reading is complex, and those studies don't provide context. It requires more than the understanding of how the English language works and the theorization about the most effective way to teach it. Curriculums, approaches, and programs have to include, and address, the social/emotional aspect of dyslexia. The adults represented in this book rarely included any part of the official definition when they described dyslexia. Additionally, dyslexia in adults does look a little different than it does in children. Many adults have been able to become proficient in the areas typically deficient in dyslexics, but they still struggle with spelling and fluency rates.

- *Modify the definition.* The current definition falls short in considering the emotional toll dyslexia can have on an individual. An intervention that responds only to the symptoms listed in the definition without addressing the emotional toll will not be as effective as it could be.

How do we teach self-advocacy?

Teaching self-advocacy skills should begin no later than the end of elementary school (age ten). This advocacy training has to be done by parents and teachers. There are more students without advocates, so if the school creates an environment where the students can have a voice, they will have fewer casualties. Before a person can self-advocate, they have to have a deep understanding of what dyslexia is and how it affects them. That can be done only if we use the word *dyslexia* and if we explain it as honestly as possible.

Once they have that understanding, they can begin to learn how to self-advocate. They also need to understand that their self-advocacy helps not only them, but also other students who cannot self-advocate, which can be motivational. To begin this process, students should be aware of whether or not they have a diagnosis and whether or not they have an IEP or 504.[1] This information will inform how and what they advocate for. The most important thing they will advocate for is their accommodations, and they have to become experts in explaining why they need them.

Student self-advocacy can take several forms, but some organizations do offer coursework, like the Dyslexia Training Institute's Virtual Student Academy, which offers a class for students over the summer. The following steps are suggested as ways to help students become their own advocates:

1. Use the word *dyslexia* and use it a lot. Teach them what dyslexia is and what it is not. Help them discover some role models with dyslexia.
2. Teach students how to create an "elevator speech" about what dyslexia is and is not. They can practice this speech so that they can use it to talk to their teachers, family members, friends, and everyone else about their dyslexia.

---

1   504 refers to Section 504 of the Rehabilitation Act. It generally gives a student access to accommodations in the classroom.

3. Make a list of common misconceptions people have about dyslexia, and work with students to practice how to respond to these misconceptions. For example, when someone says something like "Dyslexia is seeing words backwards," the student can practice their response, which should include an explanation about why that is not true.

4. If the student has an IEP or 504, sit with the student and make sure they understand what an IEP and/or 504 is and why they have it. Educate them about how and why an IEP or 504 protects their rights to learn to read and spell, and explain how to talk to their teachers about what is in their IEP.

5. Work with the student to determine which accommodations are best for them and their academic needs.

Which accommodations work the best?

For many adults with dyslexia, accommodations helped them get through school. But allowing students to provide an accurate representation of what they understand instead of being hindered by written language is more important than getting through school, and accommodations support this. There are several popular accommodations for students with dyslexia.

- *Speech-to-text.* This allows students to show the mastery of what they're writing about without being hindered by spelling. They're more likely to use complex sentence structures and higher-level vocabulary with this type of accommodation.

- *Text-to-speech.* The ability to listen to text is a gateway to higher-level information. Many students with dyslexia are relegated to books with simpler vocabulary, and they are intellectually capable of understanding higher-level topics.
- *Keyboarding.* Many people with dyslexia also have dysgraphia, a learning disorder characterized by trouble with the production of writing. Beginning keyboarding as soon as possible can make writing a far less frustrating experience for students with dyslexia and let them showcase their intellectual capability when letter formation is not a hindrance.
- *More time on tests and assignments.* Having more time to read, especially as students get into the higher grades, will help a dyslexic student demonstrate what they really know versus what they can do in a shorter amount of time.
- *Do not mark off for spelling.* Evaluate writing based on the content. If spelling is an issue, choose certain spelling patterns that the student has worked on previously, but don't litter the entire paper with red ink.
- *Take pictures of the board and supply notes.* It can be incredibly difficult for some dyslexics to listen to a lecture and simultaneously take notes. Allowing them to take a picture of the board and/or providing the notes ahead of time will allow them to absorb the content being taught.

Importance of accommodations

> I can't take notes so I wouldn't be capable of— I can't go to classes when I was younger and not now [sic]. Now I couldn't be bothered, but when I was younger I would've loved to have gone and done some sort of extracurricular activity. I would've liked to have done classes, but I couldn't take notes because I couldn't—at the time, I tried to spell the first little piece of information, the lecturer was already 20 minutes into the conversation. I'd lost it. So, there was no way. Writing that stuff was beyond me, so I just stopped. So I never did anything like that.   **Philomena**

Last but not least, students with dyslexia should never be required to read in front of their peers; they can do so when they feel ready to volunteer. Accommodations are often the saving grace for struggling students, and their importance cannot be understated.

Parting Thoughts

This is a book of stories of more than 50 adults with dyslexia, but the number of adults with similar experiences and stories is endless. Growing up with dyslexia is not an uncommon experience, but it is relatively uncommon to properly identify and teach these students. The adults in this book are all survivors, but more importantly, they are advocates. Advocates are people who add their voice to a discussion in order to make it better, or right. They shared their stories because they want to make the world a better place and they know how much better this world could be if those who are struggling are given an equal opportunity to thrive in school. They want others with dyslexia to believe in themselves and to understand that it is not their fault that those who are in charge of their education might not understand their struggle.

Many of the adults were able to succeed. Their success does not mean that they are not scarred or they don't wish their school experience was different. Here is what they might tell their ten-year-old selves:

Keep your dreams alive! Don't let people tell you that you can't follow your dreams. Hopefully school gets a little easier as you learn to cope with your dyslexia. Find someone who can help you and understands how you learn. **Natalee**

The dyslexia experience could be so different. The brave adults in this book described so many internally harrowing days at school—but it doesn't have to be that way. All they needed was one or two people who understood and advocated for them. They needed a safe place where teachers understood why they were struggling. They needed a school culture where the other students also understood them. This isn't a monumental ask when we consider that 10–15% percent of the population is dyslexic. However, it can only happen when we acknowledge the existence of dyslexia, the experience of dyslexia, and the potential of dyslexics. As one adult put it:

You just never know what that student will become. **Tim**

Resources

Books: advocacy

Dyslexia Advocate!: How to Advocate for a Child with Dyslexia within the Public Education System, by Kelli Sandman-Hurley.

7 Steps for Success: High School to College Transition Strategies for Students with Disabilities, by Elizabeth C. Hamblin.

All About IEPs, by Peter Wright, Pamela Darr Wright, and Sandra Webb O'Connor.

Special Education Law, by Peter Wright and Pamela Darr Wright.

When the School Says No, How to Get the Yes!: Securing Special Education Services for Your Child, by Vaughn Lauer.

Wrightslaw: All About Tests and Assessments, by Melissa Lee Farrall and Pamela Darr Wright.

Wrightslaw: From Emotions to Advocacy: The Special Education Survival Guide, by Peter Wright and Pamela Darr Wright.

Books: dyslexia

Dyslexia and Spelling: Making Sense of it All, by Kelli Sandman-Hurley.

The Dyslexia Empowerment Plan: A Blueprint for Renewing Your Child's Confidence and Love of Learning, by Ben Foss.

Essentials of Dyslexia Assessment and Intervention, by Nancy Mather and Barbara J. Wendling.

Overcoming Dyslexia: A New and Complete Science-Based Program for Reading Problems at any Level, by Sally Shaywitz.

Proust and the Squid: The Story and Science of the Reading Brain, by Maryanne Wolf.

Reading in the Brain: The New Science of How We Read, by Stanislaus Dehaene.

Dyslexia: websites

British Dyslexia Association—www.bdadyslexia.org.uk

Decoding Dyslexia (this website provides links to current advocacy efforts in different states and countries)—www.decodingdyslexia.net.

Dyslexia Help—www.dyslexiahelp.umich.edu

Dyslexia Training Institute—www.dyslexiatraininginstitute.org

Embracing Dyslexia—www.embracingdyslexia.com

International Dyslexia Association—www.interdys.org

Learning Ally—www.learningally.org

NoticeAbility—www.noticeability.org
    Super Dville—www.superdville.com

TED-Ed, What is Dyslexia:—www.youtube.com/watch?v=zafiGBrFkRM

Understood—www.understood.org

Wrightslaw—www.wrightslaw.com

The Yale Center for Dyslexia & Creativity—www.dyslexia.yale.edu

Simulation kits

Dyslexia for a Day Simulation Kit, produced by Dyslexia Training Institute— www.dyslexiatraininginstitute.org/simulation-kit.html

How Difficult Can This Be? The FAT City Workshop with Rick Lavoie, produced by PBS—www.ricklavoie.com/videos.html

Advocacy services

Dyslexia Training Institute, four-week course and certificate program available—www.dyslexiatraininginstitute.org

IEP Help—www.iephelp.com

Podcasts

The Dyslexia Buzz: https://thedyslexiabuzz.buzzsprout.com

Empower Dyslexia: www.empowerdyslexia.org

Adult literacy

Commission on Adult Basic Education (COABE): https://coabe.org

Grammarly: www.grammarly.com

ProLiteracy: www.proliteracy.org

References

Alexander-Passe, N. (2018) 'Dyslexia, Traumatic Schooling and Career Success: Investigating the motivations of why many individuals with developmental dyslexia are successful despite experiencing traumatic schooling.' Doctoral thesis, University of Sunderland.

Camp, M. (2015) 'What Dyslexia Really is!' Accessed on 20 April 2021 at https://discover.hubpages.com/education/What-Dyslexia-Really-is#comment-16680551.

Hicks, J. (2019) 'Dyslexia & Self-Esteem: The Hidden Mental Health Challenge.' Accessed on 20 April 2021 at www.linkedin.com/pulse/dyslexia-self-esteem-hidden-mental-health-challenge-john-hicks.

Hilden, K. & Jones, J. (2012) 'A literacy spring cleaning: Sweeping round robin reading out of your classroom.' *Reading Today*, April/May.

IDA (2020) 'Dyslexia Assessment: What Is It and How Can It Help?' Accessed on 20 April 2021 at https://dyslexiaida.org/dyslexia-assessment-what-is-it-and-how-can-it-help-2.

IDA (2021) 'Definition of Dyslexia' Accessed on 20 April 2021 at https://dyslexiaida.org/definition-of-dyslexia.

Maslow, A. H. (1943) 'A theory of human motivation.' *Psychological Review 50*, 4, 370–396.

Optiz, M. F. & Rasinski, T. (2008) *Good-bye Round Robin, Updated Edition: 25 Effective Oral Reading Strategies*. Portsmouth, NH: Heinemann.

Sandman-Hurley, K. (2016) *Dyslexia Advocate!: How to Advocate for a Child with Dyslexia within the Public Education System*. London and Philadelphia, PA: Jessica Kingsley Publishers.

Sandman-Hurley, K. (2019) *Dyslexia and Spelling*. London and Philadelphia, PA: Jessica Kingsley Publishers.

Appendix

Interview questions

- How would you describe your dyslexia?
- What is your first memory of struggling in school?
- Do you think spelling is important?
- Do you think dyslexia is a gift?
- How does dyslexia affect your daily life?
- What is your earliest memory of school struggle? What did it feel like, how do you deal with those emotions?
- What helped you in school?
- What didn't help you in school?
- Who had the biggest impact on you?
- Who or what helped you the least?
- When did you realize/find out you had dyslexia?
- What strategies do you now use to help with literacy-related tasks?
- How has dyslexia impacted your ability to help your own children?
- What advice would you give a child currently struggling in school?
- What advice would you give to a parent whose child is currently struggling?

- What advice would you give to teachers?
- Do you think spelling is important? Has spelling ever stopped you from doing something or caused you embarrassment?
- Do you prefer *dyslexic* or *person with dyslexia*?

Index